Texas Smoke

Texas Smoke

Muzzle-Loaders on the Frontier

C. F. Eckhardt

Illustrated by
Wesley G. Williams

Texas Tech University Press

This book was set in Adobe Garamond and Tango. The paper used in this book meets the minimum requirements of ANSI/NISO Z39.48-1992 (R1997).∞

Printed in the United States of America

Design by Bryce Burton

Library of Congress Cataloging-in-Publication Data
Eckhardt, C. F. (Charley F.)
    Texas smoke : muzzle-loaders on the frontier / by C. F. Eckhardt ; illustrated by Wesley G. Williams.
        p. cm.
    Includes bibliographical references (p.   ).
    ISBN 0-89672-439-5
    1. Muzzle-loading firearms—Texas—History.   I. Title.
TS535.8.E25 2001
683.4—dc21
                                                00-011141

01 02 03 04 05 06 07 08 09 / 9 8 7 6 5 4 3 2 1

Texas Tech University Press
Box 41037
Lubbock, Texas 79409-1037 USA

1-800-832-4042

ttup@ttu.edu

http://www.ttup.ttu.edu

Contents

The Guns of Texas
from the Beginning to 1860

Once, a very long time ago, I stood in front of a display case at the Texas Memorial Museum in Austin, staring at a ball-butted wheel-lock pistol. I wondered how it worked, but when I asked, no one could tell me. To the young people of Texas today who stand in similar places, wonder the same things, and still get no answers, this book is dedicated.

C. F. Eckhardt

Chapter 1

Why Guns?

The first permanent settlers to North America were the Spanish, led by a Genoese sea captain named Cristóbal Colón, a.k.a. Christopher Columbus. His three ships—the Niña, the Pinta, and the Santa Maria—anchored off a tiny, low-lying island that Colón named San Salvador and that has, today, been pretty well identified as an uninhabited key called Samana Cay. This was the beginning of the massive European settlement of the New World.

The Spanish, and those who followed, brought two things with them that helped to tame the wilderness: horses to carry them faster and farther than the Indians had ever dreamed people could travel on land, and the weapon that so terrified the Indians that they ran away at the sound of it—the gun.

In terms of power and accuracy, the guns the early settlers brought with them to North America were not a bit better than the Indians' bows. In fact, even in the fifteenth century there were better weapons available to the Europeans than the arquebus (what we now call a musket). For instance, the English longbow was a far better weapon than any early gun. Standard longbow practice range was two hundred paces, which might have been anywhere from 130 yards to 220 yards, depending on who did the pacing. The standard target was a butt, which was the bottom of a beer keg, about two feet across. A good longbowman was expected to hit the butt "more often than not," which might have been fifty-one arrows out of a hundred but was probably considerably better than that. While an individual longbowman shooting at a still target could hit it regularly at one hundred yards, and make it hunt cover even if he missed at two hundred, the secret of a longbow's success on the battlefield was not in the ability of a single archer to hit a single target, but in the ability of a hundred or a thousand or more archers to put flights of arrows one after another in the air and have them hit in a very small space—say, a circle forty feet across—at great ranges.

A good longbow will cast a well-fletched and well-balanced r row four hundred yards or even more. At that range, any good longbowman could put six arrows in the air before the first one hit, and all of his arrows would hit pretty much in that same forty-foot circle. The English longbow made its reputation not with Robin Hood-style trick shooting but at places like Agincourt, where thousands of longbowmen rained thousands of arrows on masses of horsemen or infantry at great ranges and in a short time.

Suppose, for a moment, that you're the commander of an army in the field. You have about a thousand infantrymen armed with swords and pikes and similar weapons, and five hundred horsemen, knights in full armor. You also have a thousand good longbowmen. Across the field, about four hundred yards away, your enemy has his army—three thousand infantry armed like yours, and fifteen hundred knights. He has no longbowmen.

You're in trouble, it seems. He outnumbers you three to one in both infantry and cavalry, and if you close with him on the field without doing something about that he's going to stomp all over you. You do, however, have those longbow-men. Can they help?

You bet they can! You order them to open fire, targeted on the enemy's knights. Inside a minute, something like ten thousand steel-pointed arrows are raining all over the enemy knights, and if only one out of ten drops a man or a horse, you've evened the odds in cavalry. Once you've done that, you have them switch targets to the infantry, which wears much lighter armor than the knights—no steel boilerplate here. Most of the infantry will be wearing something like a quilted cotton jacket or maybe one of stiff leather, and all it will protect, most likely, will be the soldier's chest. That and a helmet or an iron or leather war cap will be the only armor the foot soldiers have. Arrows will be far more effective against them than against the knights. You can look for three or four out of every ten arrows to take out men. When your bowmen rain twenty to thirty thousand arrows on the infan-try, you've done a lot better than even the odds, you've won the battle. That's how the English used longbows, and that's what made them so feared all over Europe.

There was an even better weapon available for shooting at individual targets, and the Spanish had it and used it. A simple hunting crossbow, cocked by hand or a goatsfoot cocking lever, shooting a light arrow or quarrel no longer than a person's forearm, was about half again as accurate on individual targets as was a longbow. It took only a few weeks to learn to shoot well, while it took a lifetime to make a good longbowman. An arbalest, or war crossbow, was something else again. The bow was usually a tempered steel spring (I've seen one made from an old automobile leaf spring, and a fearsomely powerful thing it was, with the ability to drive a heavy, steel-headed bolt or quarrel completely through a four-inch board at fifty yards) strung with a heavy, twisted rawhide, sinew-reinforced bowstring usually strengthened further with iron wire. It was cocked with a gearbox affair or a windlass, because it was so strong it would tire the bowman out to have to cock it with his hands. Some of them were so strong they couldn't be cocked by hand. It took a while to cock and load—a half-dozen good longbowmen could chew up a whole company of arbalesters while they were cocking and loading for a second shot—but the thing was deadly accurate on a man-sized target out to three hundred yards. At half that distance, it would drive a steel-headed quarrel completely through the heaviest plate armor.

Now, ironically, had the Spaniards, and later the English and French, been armed with these powerful, accurate, long-ranged weapons instead of primitive guns, the Indians might well have made dog meat out of the conquistadores and later the settlers. Arbalests, trebuchets, mangonels, ballistae, springals, and the other noted weapons of the Middle Ages were far more powerful than the arquebuses and artillery pieces (usually sakers, demisakers, and falconets rather than cannons, since the artillery pieces known as cannons were too heavy to drag around) but they wouldn't have bothered the Indians nearly as much. Apart from the twang of a bowstring, the sizzle or swish of an arrow, or the crunch of a falling boulder, these weapons were quiet, as were the Indians' own weapons. The advantage guns had was noise.

Crossbowman on left crouches behind his shield to reload, using a puller. Crossbowman on right has a windlass on his belt for reloading.

You might say, and you wouldn't be far wrong, that the Spaniards and the other early settlers simply scared more Indians with noise than they ever shot with bullets. The tremendous bang, the flash, and the smoke of a primitive gun, if you've never seen one, will scare even a modern person who has seen and heard a modern gun fire. The Indians had never seen or heard a gun of any kind.

I don't pull this idea out of thin air. Back in 1554, three Spanish ships wrecked on Padre Island, on the lower coast of Texas, during a storm. The survivors, about fifty men, women, and children, tried to walk back to Mexico. They salvaged swords, daggers, crossbows, and quarrels, but no guns and no powder.

Four made it. While the Spaniards killed attacking Indians at ranges far greater than the primitive guns would have, the Indians had them for lunch. (This may literally be the truth; the Indians they fought were Karankawas, who were cannibals.) As it turns out, the range and accuracy of the crossbows didn't bother the Indians nearly as much as the blast of a gun would have, even if the shot missed. The annals of early exploration—not just Spanish, English, French, and Portuguese, but American as well—are full of tales of Indians running away and hiding at the sound of a gun.

From Columbus's arrival in the New World in 1492 until the beginning of the Civil War in 1861, guns changed but little. Juan Soldado, the foot soldier who followed Spanish conquistador Hernán Cortés in 1517, loaded his matchlock arquebus by pouring a mixture of sulfur, saltpeter, and charcoal down the barrel from the front, dropped a lead shot on top of it, and stuck fire from an outside source into the powder to fire the weapon. Johnny Reb and Billy Yank, when they met for the first time at Manassas Junction in 1861, nearly 350 years later, were still doing the same thing.

If we had a time machine with which we could snatch Juan from Cortés's army and pull him forward to 1861—provided he didn't die of fright—once we explained the workings of a percussion cap to him and he learned to hold Johnny's Enfield or Billy's Springfield against his shoulder rather than his chest, he could fire the percussion musket as easily as his matchlock. If, however, we were to pull him forward another two years to 1863 and hand him one of Christopher Spencer's or B. Tyler Henry's cartridge-loading repeaters and a box of cartridges, he'd be completely lost.

Eighteen-sixty was a watershed year in the history of guns. It was in that year that the muzzle-loading gun dominated the American frontier for the last time. By 1865, when Robert E. Lee's gray-clad soldiers marched away from Appomattox Courthouse, the muzzle-loader as a practical weapon of war and conquest, even of hunting and self-protection, was dead. The rest of the American frontier period belonged to the cartridge gun.

Chapter 2

Matchlocks and Gunpowder

The Spanish arquebus that Juan Soldado carried as he followed Cortés and Pizarro, and later Coronado and de Oñate, across the Americas, was about as simple a gun as could be made. It was a large iron or steel tube, closed at one end except for a small hole to admit fire. It was attached by iron or brass bands to a stock that looked a lot like a mill-run two-by-four and wasn't a lot more finely finished. It was simple and cheap to make. Because Spain, in particular, always considered the New World a backwater and a dumping ground, it hung on here a long time after better, more modern guns replaced it in Europe. It had only one moving part. The serpentine or triggering mechanism, which was shaped like an *S* but elongated and with less bend at the ends, held a length of treated rope called a slow match in one end. When the other end was pressed upwards against the stock, the fire-end brought the coal on the end of a smoldering slow match in contact with the vent or touch-hole, which led to the powder.

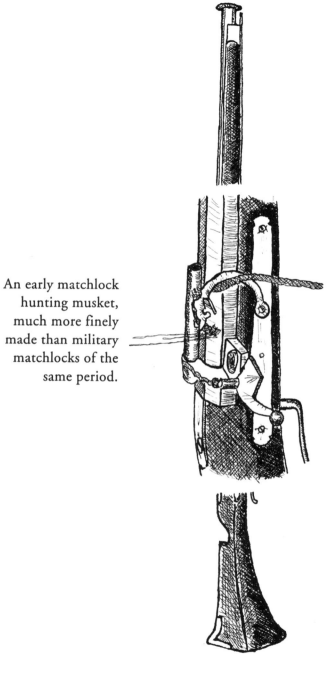

An early matchlock
hunting musket,
much more finely
made than military
matchlocks of the
same period.

Generally around the touch-hole there was a raised lip, called a pan, and into this pan Juan had put some extra powder. When the glowing end of the slow match came into contact with the powder in the pan, the powder flashed up, lit off the powder charge inside the gun barrel, and with luck fired the arquebus.

To load his arquebus, Juan Soldado took a measured amount of gunpowder, poured it down the barrel from the muzzle, followed it either with a lead ball weighing as much as two ounces or with a handful of buckshot, stuffed in a wad of paper or rag or maybe a handful of cotton or wool lint—sometimes even some grass if nothing else was handy—took a long metal or wooden stick called a ramrod off his back or out of his belt, and rammed or tamped the whole mess solidly in the barrel. The gun was then loaded, but it was a long way from being ready to shoot.

Before Juan could fire, he had to light his slow match. He unwound the chemically treated rope he usually carried wrapped around his hat or helmet—sometimes under the brim or inside the helmet if the weather was bad—struck flint and steel to make a spark, and blew on the tip of the slow match to make sure it was going once he got the sparks to it. He'd then generally spin the lighted end around in the air above his head to make sure it was fanned up into a good coal and wouldn't go out on him. Once he had it going, he hung it over his shoulder, fire behind him, where it just might set fire to his pants while he was doing everything else.

Once the slow match was lit, he had to secure his rest, which was a long stick with a metal spike on one end and a metal fork on the other. He rammed the spike in the ground and laid the arquebus in the fork, muzzle toward the enemy, took the small metal cover off the pan, and pulled a wooden

Spanish private soldier from the conquistador period loading his wheel-lock arquebus.

plug called a tompion out of the muzzle. These things kept the powder from getting damp—some of the time.

Now he took a small brass, horn, or gourd bottle, poured a small amount of powder in the pan, and put the cover back on. Then he clipped his slow match, coal end first, into the serpentine, slapped out the fire it had started on his pants, knocked the ash off the slow match and made sure it was properly adjusted, uncovered the pan, rested the butt of the weapon against the middle of his chest, took aim as well as he could (the arquebus had no sights) and squeezed the back end of the serpentine up against the stock. This brought the coal on the slow match into the powder in the pan, and about three times out of four there was a sputter, followed by a tremendous KA-WHOOM! and poor Juan staggered back about three or four steps from the kick of the thing.

Juan's individual bullet was unlikely to hit anything more than thirty or so yards away if he was firing by himself. The bows used by the Indians covered at least this distance, and these bows weren't nearly as powerful nor nearly as accurate as the English longbows. If Juan and fifty or a hundred other arquebusiers all fired at once in the same direction, however, they put a lot of lead in the air, and some of it was bound to hit the target. Volley fire was not only unbelievably noisy but put a curtain of shot in the air that could be effective as far as one hundred yards away or more, when the guns were loaded with ball. While buckshot wasn't quite as long-ranged, the effect was much greater. A hundred arquebusiers who stood their ground and fired a volley of buckshot into five times that many charging horsemen could usually win their part of the battle with a single volley.

The gunpowder Juan charged his arquebus with was, at that time and for many years to come, the only thing you

Spanish soldier
(around 1500) with
matchlock arquebus
primed and loaded,
almost ready to fire,
using slow match.

could use to fire a gun, so it would be wise to take a hard look at it. Gunpowder, also called black powder to distinguish it from the white or smokeless gunpowder used to load modern guns (which is neither white nor completely smokeless), is very old, far older than most folks think. "Magic dust" containing at least sulfur and saltpeter appears to have been used as early as ancient Egypt, helping priests and magicians scare folks out of their bedsheets. "Bryngynge fourthe ye daemon mydst ye clowdes of fowle-smellynge smoak" can be done very neatly by scattering a handful of sulfur/saltpeter mixture on a convenient fire—and what's a wizard without a fire?—and having a suitably costumed assistant step from behind a curtain while the audience is wheezing, coughing, and wiping their eyes.

With the exception of "maykynge ye coloured fyres" and producing "fowle-smellynge smoak," gunpowder's properties went unappreciated until the Chinese discovered them. About A.D. 150, a Chinese general used something he called "earth thunder," which from the description seems to have been buried barrels of gunpowder with long fuses laid to them, to stop an invading army by having the ground blow up in their faces. By the fifth century, the Chinese were regularly using firecrackers in celebrations.

While the ancient Chinese made their firecrackers with black powder, modern ones are made with something else entirely. Mostly they contain powdered magnesium or flash powder, with just enough potassium perchlorate to make a bang. Potassium perchlorate is almost unbelievably powerful and dangerous in large amounts. It absolutely cannot be made safe enough to use to load any kind of a gun. It will blow the gun apart—and probably the person holding it as well. If you've ever had a Black Cat firecracker go off in your hand, you know how much your hand hurt afterwards. A Black Cat contains about enough of the powder used in modern firecrackers to cover the nail on your little finger. It would take two or three hundred times that much to make a regular musket load, and because the powder is so powerful, it would blow the musket up in your face.

In the thirteenth century, Subodai Khan, general of the Golden Horde of Ogadai Khan, used gunpowder-fueled war rockets against European armies just before breaking off the invasion of Europe and returning to China at Ogadai's death. When these rockets hit the ground, they broke open and gave off a foul, choking smoke that "maddened men and horses." While this sounds like it might have been tear gas, it was probably the smoke from burning sulfur.

Gunpowder came to Europe late. The great Scottish wizard, Michel le Scotte, whom we call Michael Scott today, and who was born about 1175 and died about 1234 (both dates have question marks after them in the encyclopedia), seems to have been familiar enough with "ye magickal fyres" of sulfur, saltpeter, and charcoal to name the three "Satan's trinity." His pupil, Roger Bacon, left a coded reference in his notes which just might prove to be, if the notes are ever correctly decoded, an early formula for gunpowder. We know that in A.D. 1346, at a place called Crécy, France, in a battle between the English and the French, the English used the first guns ever mentioned in European history, but it was the longbow and not guns that won the battle for the English at Crécy, as it would win many more before guns became good enough to make a difference in warfare.

We know now, of course, that there is nothing magical or supernatural about what gunpowder does, but for many years people believed that the stuff exploded because it contained fearsome demons, which made it go BANG! and stink like—well, like the fires of Hell were supposed to stink. If these demons weren't immediately killed after doing their work (making the gunpowder explode), they would run loose all over the countryside in the manner of demons and blight the crops, sour the milk, and make folks sick. Special priests and sometimes self-appointed wizards made a pretty good thing out of jobs in powdermills, where they recited special prayers or worked special magic that was supposed to kill the demons in the explosion. A good description of this practice can be found in science-fiction writer H. Beam Piper's *Lord Kalvan of Otherwhen.* Piper also has quite a lot to say about guns and gun making.

Black powder is a simple mechanical mixture of three pretty common chemicals: saltpeter, sulfur, and charcoal. Although the latter is much like that used to cook on the backyard grill, proper charcoal for gunpowder should be made from willow or alder wood rather than from oak, hickory, or mesquite.

Getting the ingredients together could be quite a trick. Potassium nitrate, or saltpeter, is a salt produced in the decomposition of animal waste products. It was once called "ye whyte effenfe of ye dungge." Saltpeter was most commonly found by tearing down long-standing piles of manure, called dung heaps or dung hills, which were a fixture on farms in the days before chemical fertilizers. Farmers, in those days, went around their farms with a cart and a shovel and loaded up all the dung or manure they found, then put it in a big pile, which for obvious reasons was usually kept downwind of the house. When the fields needed fertilizing in the spring, the farmer loaded his manure cart from his dung heap and spread it on the fields.

When the dung heap was pulled down, the ground beneath it contained grayish, rock-like lumps of a gritty-feeling substance. These lumps were crude saltpeter, leached out of the manure by rain and time. The lumps were crushed, sifted, and washed, and finally the powder was dissolved in water, then precipitated out and dried. The result was a clean, white, salty-looking, salty-tasting powder used in medicines and in preserving meat. If a lot of it was needed at once—say, a war was coming on—it could be leached out of animal waste. Bat guano is particularly rich in it. A powder maker who had access to a bat cave was especially well supplied with saltpeter. He might even sell his saltpeter to other powder makers or trade it for sulfur.

Also called brimstone, sulfur was the hardest one of Satan's trinity to find, although it was pretty much the easiest to process once a source had been found, generally a spring of foul-smelling water. To get the sulfur out of the water—sulfur, of course, is what made it stink—you filled a shallow pan with the water and set it over a slow fire, making sure the water evaporated quickly without boiling. If it boiled, the sulfur would be lost in the steam, while in evaporation it would gather in the pan.

After you evaporated many, many pans of stinking water, you'd begin to notice a vague discoloration, a yellow line around the edge or brim of the pan. After you evaporated pan after pan day and night for a week or so, this line would begin to thicken into a hard, stone-like deposit called brimstone, because it forms at the brim of the pan. The deposit was bright yellow—the sulfur you were after.

Once you had enough of a deposit, you would flake it off into a mortar and "allow" your assistant to grind it to a fine powder while you made some more. It might take days or even months, doing it this way, to get enough sulfur for a few pounds of gunpowder. Texas has many stinking springs—once we even had a town called Stinking Springs, and we still have one called Sulfur Springs—but Europe doesn't have all that many. Some pretty fair battles got fought over control of stinking springs and sulfur supplies.

Charcoal is wood that has been turned completely to carbon by getting it hot enough to burn without giving it enough air to flame and turn to ash. An old-time charcoal burner used hardwood only: oak, ash, or later, for making gunpowder, willow or alder. He never used resinous wood like pine, hemlock, or the juniper we Texans call cedar, because it would catch fire too readily. First he set a long pole in the ground so it would stick up straight, but just deep enough so it wouldn't fall over. Around the base of this pole he laid a small fire of very dry, easily lit kindling. Against the center pole he stacked his hardwood poles, dozens of them, to make a tepee-shaped structure. He then took mud and plastered it thickly all over the tepee, until the only vents were at the top and one or two very small ones at the bottom. Once the mud was plastered on, he pulled the center pole out and dropped fire through the top onto the stuff he'd laid in the floor of the tepee. The fire would catch and begin to burn. Before it had burned out all its oxygen or burned up all its fuel, it would begin to catch the hardwood poles making up the tepee. Once the hardwood was burning, the charcoal maker sealed up the air holes almost but not quite all the way with mud, and walked away to leave the tepee for a week or so. It would burn that way, not quite enough air to flame, until the poles inside had everything burned away but the carbon. Then the charcoal burner would return, knock down the tepee and cover the remaining coals with sand, wait a day, and then sift through the sand and dirt to recover the charcoal.

Those mud-covered tepees were pretty much a fixture in hardwood forests the world over until just a very few years ago. When I was a young man, we would still see them along creek banks. Once in a while, a charcoal burner and his family would come to the ranch house and ask if we had any scrub oak we'd like to get rid of. If we did, Dad would show him where it was. The burners would set up camp, build their tepees and plaster them with mud, light the fires, and then go off to where the next stand of scrub was located. A week or so later they'd be back to gather the charcoal. Those tepees stayed mighty warm with the fires inside. On really cold days I'd sometimes get off my horse and wrap my arms around one until I warmed up.

Once a powder maker got all three ingredients, he mashed them to powder in a mortar made of something that wouldn't strike a spark—generally brass, crockery, or lignum vitae (a very hard wood). Then, in the very earliest times, he mixed equal amounts of each and presto! gunpowder. The stuff wasn't very easy to set off, it wasn't very powerful, and it left bucketsful of fouling ash in a gun barrel. It would explode, though, if you packed it so tight it couldn't do anything else.

Alchemists and wizards (those being the names for folks who messed with stuff that went BANG!) tampered with the proportions until a mixture of 75 percent saltpeter, 15 percent charcoal, and 10 percent sulfur was arrived at. In about five hundred years or so, nobody's managed to improve on the formula. An old-time powder maker mixed fifteen dippers of saltpeter, three dippers of powdered charcoal, and two dippers of sulfur, and he had gunpowder. It was called meal powder because it was as fine as meal—a little coarser than flour but not as coarse as cornmeal—and it had problems.

The saltpeter, being the heaviest ingredient, tended to sink to the bottom of the container, which spoiled the powder unless it was remixed. In meal-powder days—and Juan Soldado, following the conquistadores, probably loaded with meal powder for a long time—a soldier or hunter shook his powder flask or horn before loading up to insure the powder was properly mixed. This held on a long time after there was no more need for it. For a couple of centuries, a regular job in armories or castle magazines or on shipboard was turning the powder: tumping over the powder kegs, rolling them around a while, and then setting them up bottom upwards to remix the powder. The kegs had their ends painted different colors so that the sergeant or petty officer in charge of the powder-turning detail could tell at a glance if the soldiers or seamen assigned to the detail had actually turned the powder or had just sneaked out for a beer. Modern gunpowder comes in one-pound cans, but up until just a few years ago you could still buy it in twenty-five-pound kegs, and those kegs still had their ends painted different colors, even though there had been no reason to do that for about four hundred years.

Of course no one, absolutely no one, was ever allowed to smoke around the powder. You'll find that a lot of old soldiers—I'm proud to be one of them—still won't smoke on a firing range. Army regulations absolutely forbid it, and we just don't feel comfortable around anyone who smokes on a firing range. This goes back to the very early days of armies, when there were often open barrels or kegs of powder on the range, and a stray spark from a smoke could set off an explosion and hurt people.

Meal powder was a lot of trouble, so folks experimented with ways to make sure that the powder, once mixed, stayed mixed. The method that worked involved putting water into the powder—one old recipe I copied insisted that the only suitable water was human urine; specifically, "ye pysse of ye maydene notte yette knowynge ye manne"—and then working the mixture into a dough. The dough was then pressed into molds and allowed to dry in the sun until the molds made hard cakes. The cakes were then ground to a powder slightly coarser than coarsely ground cornmeal for the finest, and somewhat coarser than whole peppercorns for the coarsest. Later, cannon powder was made in grains as big as the last joint on a man's thumb. This was called "corned powder," and it not only stayed mixed, it was a lot more powerful than meal powder. For a long time cannons continued to use meal powder while small arms, muskets and pistols, used corned powder. When cannons finally began to use corned powder, a lot of the older ones began to explode. This made artillerymen nervous, as you might expect. It was standard practice for an artilleryman to lay a long fuse of powder from the cannon's touch-hole, light it, and dive for cover until after the shot.

Long after corned powder became common, meal powder continued to turn up in wartime, when a lot of gunpowder was needed in a hurry, since the corning process, especially the drying, took a lot of time. As late as 1588, the commander of the Spanish Armada offered a special Mass of Thanksgiving to Saint Barbara (the patroness of artillerymen, miners, powder makers, engineers, firemen, and others who deal in fire and explosives) because all the powder for the Armada was corned.

Today's black powder, just for the record, is made exactly the same way, though the drying is done under heat lamps rather than in the sun. Visiting a powder mill is like stepping two or three centuries back in time. Everything in the place, the mixing vats and paddles, the molds for caking and the rollers for grinding, even the gears that turn the machinery, are made of wood, and the whole place creaks and groans like an ungreased windmill. All this is for safety: one spark and BOOM! no powder mill. Workers in a powder mill have to wear antistatic hairspray and a special antistatic coverall instead of regular clothes. Before they go inside, a security officer checks to make sure they don't have anything with them that could cause a spark or make a fire. Visitors also have to wear the coveralls and hairspray, as well as special antistatic boots over their shoes. They are expected to turn out their pockets and empty their purses before going in, and anything like matches, a lighter, or even a metal pocketknife that might accidentally cause a spark is locked in a safe; the visitor doesn't get it back until he leaves. Black powder is awfully easy to set off. A spark of static electricity will do nicely. A powder mill explosion is a sight to see, provided you are at a safe distance, don't know anyone inside, and don't own stock in the mill. All it leaves is a big, smoky hole.

The guns the Spanish and their French rivals brought into Texas in the sixteenth and early seventeenth centuries were, for the most part, matchlocks. All, so far as we know, were smoothbore: the insides of the barrels were as smooth as a water pipe or a modern shotgun barrel. They would shoot round balls or buckshot equally well. Most were very large caliber, about the size of an eight-gauge shotgun; a thumb or big toe could fit down the barrel without getting caught. Because they were so big and kicked so hard when they were shot, most of them were fired by resting the butt against the firer's chest rather than his shoulder. One old musketry manual suggests that an arquebus should never be fired from the shoulder, because "it will be found that the shoulder cannot be moved next day." Juan Soldado rested his arquebus against his chest—he usually wore chest armor, although it was more often boiled leather or heavy quilting than steel—and staggered back two or three steps when he fired.

An eight-gauge arquebus might use 250 to 300 grains of meal powder, or as much as 200 grains of corned powder to fire its two-ounce ball. Grains, by the way, doesn't mean Juan poured the individual grains of powder out and counted them one by one. It refers to a way of measuring weight. There are seven thousand grains in a pound. In very earliest times, "one grain" meant the weight of a single grain of wheat. Powder was also measured in drachms (pronounced *drams*). One drachm of powder weighed about thirty-eight grains. The Spanish usually weighed powder in onzas, almost exactly one troy or apothecary's ounce, which is pretty close to 580 grains. A good charge of meal powder for an arquebus was "media onza," half an onza, or about 290 grains. When you realize that a ten-gauge shotgun only used ninety-five grains of powder and the biggest buffalo rifles used only about 150 grains in their most powerful shells, you can imagine how an arquebus kicked. Since Juan Soldado was, on the average, only about five feet, four inches tall and weighed around 140 pounds, shooting his arquebus was pretty hard on him. If he wasn't a very good shot, it's probably because target practice was too painful.

Chapter 3

Flint and Steel

Folks had long known how to make a spark by striking a hard rock such as flint, chert, or agate against another hard rock or a piece of steel, but meal powder is hard to set off that way, at least on purpose. (Accidentally is another story.) The best way to make sure meal powder fired was to stick a hot wire, a burning coal, or a flaming stick into it. The ignition of gunpowder by flint and steel didn't occur until corned powder became common.

The flintlock seems to have been invented in several forms, at almost the same time, in widely scattered parts of Europe, North Africa, and maybe Western Asia. Spain and the Moorish countries of North Africa produced several different kinds of flintlocks, but the two we know came to Texas are the miquelet and lazarino locks.

They both worked about the same way. A spring-loaded arm holding the flint or chert was driven against a piece of steel to make sparks, which shot into an open pan containing powder. There are differences in the way they are made and

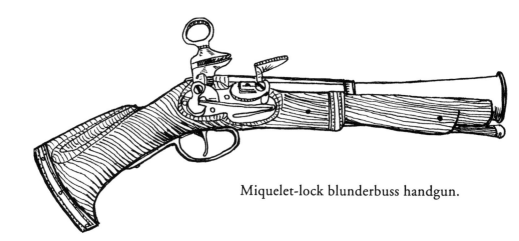

Miquelet-lock blunderbuss handgun.

in the fine points of exactly how each one works, but they aren't the sort of thing we're interested in right now.

We know both came to Texas because a lazarino lock was dug up during the archaeological investigation at La Bahía Presidio at Goliad, and three miquelet-lock muskets were found, stacked in a tripod, on a hillside near Liberty Hill, in Central Texas. It wasn't like they were lost, because they had been known for a very long time. All the wood had long since rotted away. All anyone saw was three iron pipes forming a tripod. Local folks said that there had once been a Texas Ranger camp there. On the night of July 18, 1878, when the Rangers were suddenly called to go to Round Rock to try to capture Sam Bass, the train robber, they left in such a hurry that they left their cooking tripod behind and never came back to get it.

Somebody got more curious and began to dig around the old tripod. He found, instead of a cooking tripod, three muskets: the barrels, barrel bands, locks, triggers, and butt plates. They had been there two hundred years before anyone ever heard of Sam Bass, and a hundred and fifty years before there

Spanish "Cuera" (leather) Dragoon or Presidial (fort) cavalry-
man, armed with a lance and a miquelet-lock musketoon, a
weapon shorter than a musket but longer than a carbine, with a
full musket-type stock rather than a half-barrel-length carbine
stock. He carries a thick leather shield.

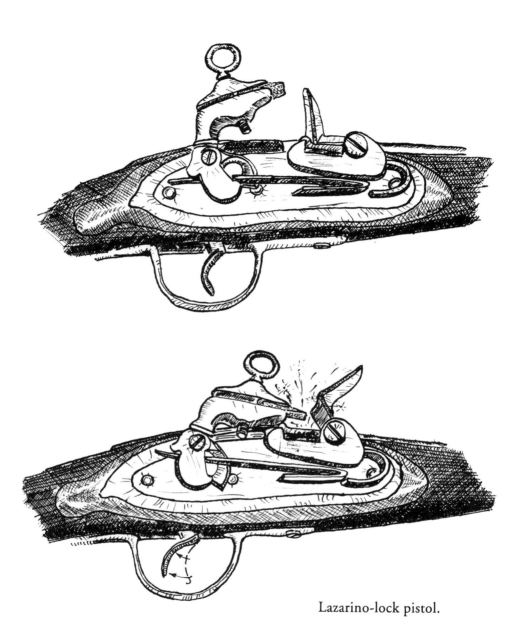

Lazarino-lock pistol.

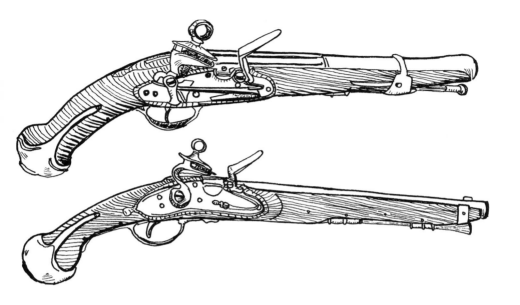

were any Texas Rangers. To this day, no one knows what happened to the men who left their muskets stacked there.

The Dutch produced a little better lock than either the lazarino or miquelet, which they called the "schnauphaunce" or "pecking hen" lock, and which we call the snaphance today. Legend says that the lock was invented by poachers, illegal night hunters who didn't want a glowing slow match on a matchlock giving them away in the dark. You have to wonder about this tale. Why didn't the Dutch poachers use crossbows or prodds (special crossbows that shot lead, stone, or clay balls instead of quarrels)? A crossbow not only doesn't have a slow match; it also doesn't go KABOOM! and make a big flash in the night. The Germans, predictably, came up with the most complicated and expensive, and at the same time the best and most reliable, gun lock using flint and steel: the wheel lock.

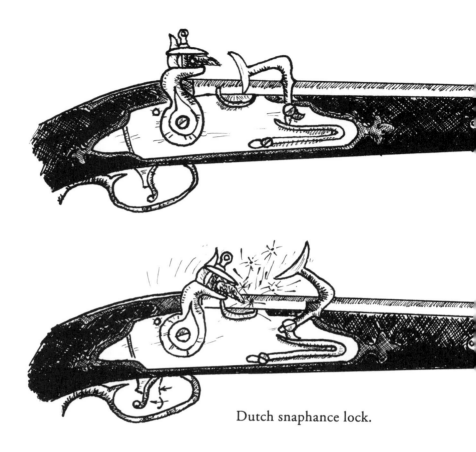

Dutch snaphance lock.

All of these things worked on the same principle as a cigarette lighter: scratch flint, agate, chert, or iron pyrite across a
piece of steel to make enough sparks to set off the powder. In
the earliest locks, like the miquelet, the lazarino, and the
snaphance, the powder was in a pan that had to be uncovered
by hand before the shot. The touch-hole was in the side of
the barrel, and the flint was held in a moveable, spring-
loaded arm called a serpentine, a cock because it was what
you pulled or "cocked" back to fire the gun, or later (and

incorrectly) a hammer. The steel was on a hinged arm above the pan called the frizzen, or sometimes the hammer; it did look something like a carpenter's hammer.

To fire the gun, the cover had to be taken off the pan by hand, the serpentine pulled back as far as it would go, the frizzen pulled forward until it hung over the pan, and the trigger squeezed. The serpentine slammed forward, the flint scraped down the frizzen, which flipped forward to keep from shattering the flint, and sparks went everywhere including, hopefully, into the powder. With luck the priming caught fire and set off the main charge and the gun fired. The odds were about one in five that it wouldn't fire, and all that would happen would be a flash in the pan. The priming powder would catch fire but fail to light the main charge; the result was a flash and a cloud of smoke from the pan. That's how the expression "a flash in the pan" came to mean something that promises to make a big bang but only makes a fizzle.

The German wheel lock worked differently and better. Wheel locks were very expensive guns, incidentally, the sort of thing a nobleman-soldier or gentleman-adventurer might carry, and they looked it. Many surviving wheel locks are finely engraved, the metal inlaid with silver and gold, the fancy wood stocks elaborately carved or inlaid with silver and gold wire, or with carved pieces of ivory or nacre (mother-of-pearl). Some have been found with the entire stock made of ivory, handsomely hand-carved to look like a hound, or with the head of a knight on the butt, or in one case I know of, carved in the shape of a beautiful and quite naked woman.

Most of the wooden-stocked wheel lock pistols, which were generally what the soldiers used, had a large ball, sometimes lead-loaded, and sometimes set with spikes like a

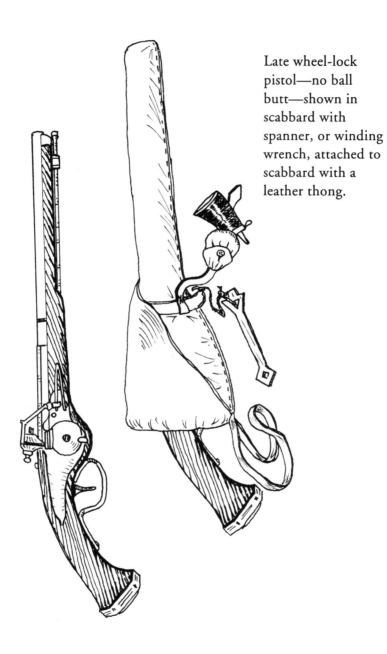

Late wheel-lock pistol—no ball butt—shown in scabbard with spanner, or winding wrench, attached to scabbard with a leather thong.

knight's mace on the butt. Particularly since the wheel lock took a while to reload and rewind, sometimes that ball came in handy. If the enemy got a little too close before a soldier was finished reloading and "spanning" (winding up) his wheel-lock pistols, he whacked the enemy with that ball. If a ball-butted wheel-lock dag, or pistol, had spikes in the ball, anybody who was whacked with it stayed whacked for quite a while.

The wheel lock itself was pretty complicated and expensive to make. It had a toothed wheel like the one on a cigarette lighter, but much larger and with larger teeth. The wheel had to be made of extremely good steel and mounted on a cogged axle. A chain was attached to the axle in such a way that the chain wrapped around the axle when the wheel was turned. A strong leaf spring was attached to the end of the chain. When the wheel was wound up with a special wrench or key, called a spanner, the chain wrapped around the axle and put tension on the spring. The trigger locked the wheel in place. The flint, held in a moveable piece called a dog (often made or engraved in the shape of a hound holding the flint in its mouth) was usually pyrites in a wheel lock. The dog was pushed down until the sparking element was touching the wheel, and then the pan was opened. When the trigger was pulled, the lock on the wheel was released. The spring pulled down on the chain and spun the wheel rapidly several times. A regular stream of sparks shot into the priming.

It sounds like it took a long time, but it didn't. The wheel spun and the gun fired faster than any firearm ever had before or ever would again, until the invention of the percussion lock. For that reason, the wheel lock hung on a long time as a hunter's gun, even after flintlocks were the most common guns in war. A flintlock or a snaphance went

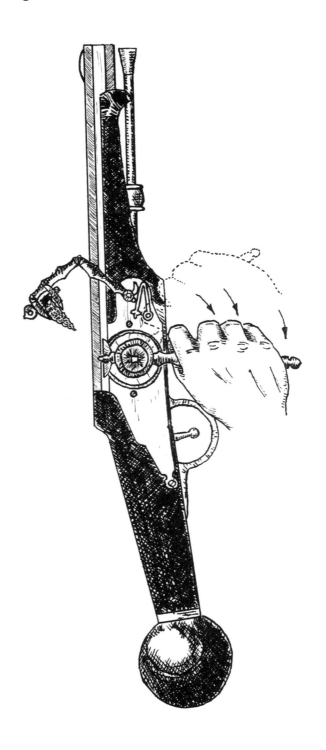

Spanning and firing
a wheel lock.

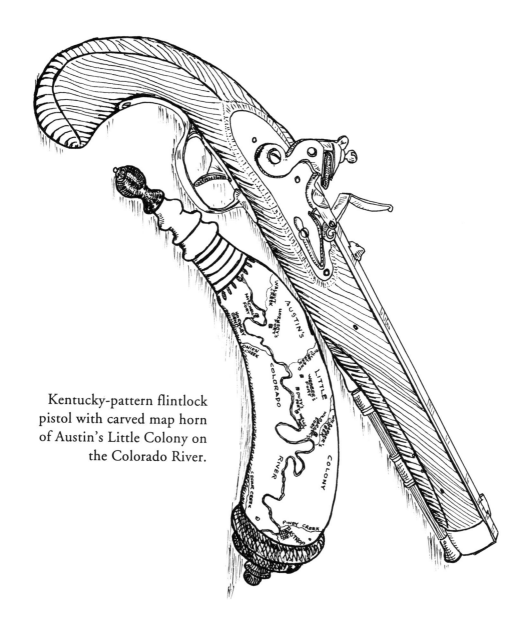

Kentucky-pattern flintlock
pistol with carved map horn
of Austin's Little Colony on
the Colorado River.

snap-whoosh-BOOM! as it fired. It might take as much as a quarter of a second to fire after the trigger was pulled. That doesn't sound like very long, but when you're trying to hold your sights on a target, particularly when someone is shooting at you, it is a very long time indeed. A wheel lock went zBOOM! in a tenth of a second or less. Besides, an early flintlock misfired about one try in five, while a wheel lock misfired only about one time in fifty.

Wheel locks didn't generally get into the hands of common soldiers, because they were very expensive. We do know, however, that some wheel locks did come to the East Coast with the English "gentlemen-adventurers" who came to dig gold and didn't find any, so it would probably be safe to assume that the young hidalgo (literally meaning "the son of something") gentlemen-adventurers who went along with the Spanish exploration parties had them as well. The French also are known to have carried wheel locks from time to time, and it's possible that one of Texas's earliest known murders—the shooting of René-Robert Cavalier, Sieur de la Salle, which happened near Navasota—was done with a wheel lock, because la Salle most likely had a wheel lock with him.

The English and the Scots took a long look at all of these systems and came up with one of their own. English and Scottish gun makers have had a long record for fine gun making. Their lock was simple and efficient without the complication and expense of the wheel lock. It was what we know, today, as the flintlock. It was to become the standard small-arms gun lock for the entire western world for nearly two hundred years.

The true flintlock, the one we call the flintlock today, is the grandson, so to speak, of the snaphance. The frizzen is attached to the rear of the pan cover and the cover is hinged at

Loading a flintlock. (1) Powder goes
down the muzzle. (2) Ball is thumb-
started into muzzle. (3) Patch is cut with
patch knife. (4) Ramrod begins ram. (5)
Ball is seated firmly on powder. (6) Pan is
primed. (7) Pistol is cocked. (8) BANG!
Note the flash from the pan.

the opposite end. When the serpentine snaps forward and the flint hits the frizzen, the frizzen snaps back and takes the pan cover with it, which uncovers the priming for the sparks. It's a little more reliable than the earlier flint mechanisms, but not as reliable as a wheel lock. It fired five times out of six on the average. It had one advantage over every other gun lock ever built: it was the first one that would work in the rain. Because the pan stayed covered until the instant of firing, the priming powder didn't have to be exposed to the weather before the trigger was pulled and therefore stayed dry. A flintlock couldn't be reloaded in the rain, but a shooter could get off one shot in anything short of a downpour, which gave the flintlock man all kinds of advantages over the feller who couldn't shoot unless the sun was shining.

The flintlock later gave the frontiersmen an advantage over the Indians, because wet weather caused Indians' rawhide and sinew bowstrings to stretch rather than bend their bows, so they couldn't shoot. Remember that old story about the Indians never attacking at night because they thought the sun god helped them in the daylight? Although some tribes believed that if they were killed at night it would be impossible to find the Happy Hunting Ground, many Indian tribes did attack at night. They didn't use bows and arrows, however; they used knives, tomahawks, and war clubs, because the dew at night got their bowstrings wet and left them unable to shoot.

In the meantime, the Germans got to playing with guns again, this time for hunting. Inside the barrels of some very heavy muskets called Jaegers (hunters), they cut spiral grooves. Originally these grooves were there to collect fouling (powder ash) so the guns could be fired more often without cleaning them, but they had an unexpected effect. If the bullet, a round lead ball, was big enough so that it fit tightly in the barrel and the little ridges of metal thrown up when the fouling grooves were cut caught hold of it, then when the gun was fired, the bullet was given a spin as it came out. A spinning bullet shot harder and straighter than one that didn't spin. Today we use the grooves not to catch powder fouling but to make the bullet spin. Long guns with rifling are called rifles.

It was sort of difficult to load a tight bullet down one of those barrels, but time wasn't all that important to a nobleman hunter, who had six or eight rifles and servants to load them for him. The Jaegers were loaded by pounding the balls down the barrel with a heavy ramrod and a big mallet.

When the Germans we now call Pennsylvania Dutch came to the Americas, they brought their heavy Jaeger rifles with them. American frontiersmen liked the accuracy of the new guns, but they didn't like the size and weight of them. Most Jaegers were very large caliber—anywhere from .69 (sixty-nine one-hundredths of an inch) to .75 (three-quarter inch) caliber—and weighed fifteen or more pounds. They used too much scarce, expensive powder and lead, and they were too heavy to tote for miles and miles in the backwoods. The Americans particularly didn't like having to drive a ball down the barrel with a hammer while a Choctaw or a Shawnee was hunting them, scalping knife in hand. The German gunsmiths who settled around Lancaster, Pennsylvania, began to do something about that.

The new rifle the Lancaster gunsmiths built for the American frontier was considerably different from the Jaeger, but kept its good points. The barrel was long and slim, generally octagonal in shape, and four feet long or even more. It was often "swamped," thinner in the middle than at

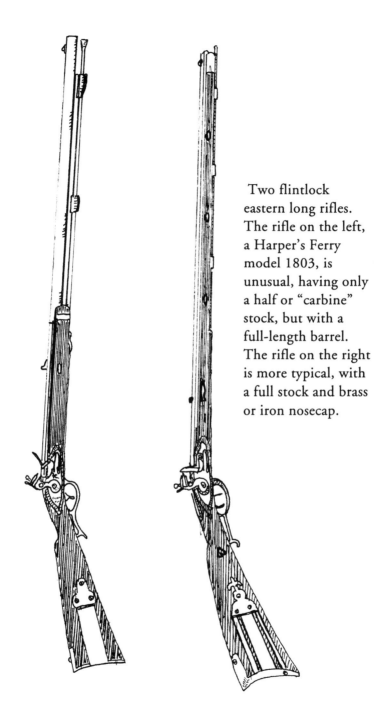

Two flintlock
eastern long rifles.
The rifle on the left,
a Harper's Ferry
model 1803, is
unusual, having only
a half or "carbine"
stock, but with a
full-length barrel.
The rifle on the right
is more typical, with
a full stock and brass
or iron nosecap.

the ends, which some men said made the sights easier to use. The stocks were usually made in one piece and extended all the way to the muzzle, a graceful, hand-carved sweep of maple or walnut that might be five and a half feet long. The lock was steel, of course, sometimes blued, sometimes color case-hardened in shades of blue, grey, brown, and red. The barrel could be blued but was usually a rich brown. The furniture—the little doodads, like the nosecap on the stock, the ramrod pipes, the trigger guard, the patchbox, the butt plate, and the counterbrace for the lock (which was really just a washer to hold the lock screws to the stock, but it could be the fanciest washer ever made)—could be of iron or steel, but were usually of brass or sometimes silver. Many of these rifles had the "modern" cheekrest on the stock, and in that cheekrest an artistic gunsmith might inlay a brass, silver, nacre, or ivory weeping heart, star, or as in one I saw in a private collection, an ivory figure of Diana, goddess of the hunt, drawing her bow, and she was plumb nekkid. You can bet that one belonged to a wealthy bachelor!

The caliber was a big difference. Jaegers were huge guns, almost as big as some small cannons. A really large-caliber Pennsylvania rifle was a .45 caliber (a little under half an inch), most were .36 caliber, and some were as small as .28 caliber—pea-ball squirrel guns, they were called. Later, as frontiersmen moved west, the gunsmiths built shorter, heavier-barreled, larger-caliber rifles with stocks that came only halfway down the barrel. These plains rifles were usually .50 caliber (half-inch) to .60 caliber, and were used to hunt buffalo and grizzly bears rather than the deer and black bears of the eastern woods. They were otherwise very similar to the "long rifles" we call Pennsylvania or Kentucky rifles today. The name Kentucky long rifle, or Kaintuck, comes from the fact that Kentucky "long hunters" men like Daniel Boone and Simon Kenton who went on hunts that might last a year or more used them. Despite the name, nearly all of these rifles were made in Pennsylvania.

Another big difference was the way they were loaded. Instead of hammering the ball down the barrel with a mallet, long rifles and, later, plains rifles were loaded with a ball slightly smaller than the bore. A .45-caliber rifle might load a .44-caliber or a .43-caliber ball; a .36-caliber rifle used a true .36-caliber ball—one that was thirty-six one-hundredths of an inch—because the bore diameter of a .36 caliber was actually 375/1000 or nearly a full .38 caliber; and a .28 caliber took a .25-caliber ball. The ball was wrapped in a piece of greased cotton or linen cloth or a piece of thin-scraped buckskin. The wrapping or patch caught the rifling and spun the ball as it came out. It slid down the barrel with only slightly more effort than it took to load a smoothbore musket.

A lot of people never referred to a gun by caliber at all, but by the number of bullets to fit it that could be cast from a single pound of lead. A man might say his rifle "throws forty to the pound," which meant forty round balls to fit it could be cast from a pound of lead. This is also the way "gauge" for shotguns is determined. A sixteen-gauge shotgun throws sixteen to the pound; that is, a pound of lead will produce sixteen round balls the size of the shotgun's bore. A twelve-gauge throws twelve to the pound, while a twenty-gauge throws twenty to the pound, and so forth. A .410 shotgun, by the way, is not a true gauge but rather a caliber, but it isn't, really, the right caliber designation. A .410 will chamber and fire a standard .44 special cartridge for a pistol, although it isn't a good idea to shoot one in it because the slug will tear up the choke coming out. A .44-caliber rifle isn't really a .44

caliber, either—it's a .429 caliber, which is really a .43, but for some reason "my trusty forty-three" just doesn't sound quite right. If we follow this road any farther we'll arrive in the State of Confusion, because in calibers almost nothing is what it's supposed to be.

It behooved young ladies to keep a close watch on their linen petticoats and other "unmentionables" when a rifleman visited the homestead, by the way. Linen was the very best material for rifle patches, and it was hard to come by on the frontier. A long hunter wasn't above snitching a linen petticoat or pair of linen underdrawers, for they would furnish him with rifle patches for many a long month.

There are all sorts of stories about the wonderful range and accuracy of the long rifle, but that's just what most of them are—stories. The best range for accurate shooting with a long rifle was sixty yards. That had to do, in part, with a strange phenomenon that sometimes occurred when round balls were shot from rifles: the balls curved in flight. Now, this didn't happen every time a rifle was fired. It seems to have been limited to eastern long rifles, which were generally a fairly small caliber, .36 to .45, and used to hunt game like deer and black bear. It did, apparently, happen often enough that riflemen knew not to bet their lives or the winter meat supply on it *not* happening. For that reason, the usual maximum range at which they shot at anything man-sized with a reasonable expectation of hitting it was considered to be 120 to 125 yards. Shooting farther than that was, in a sense, like trying to fill an inside straight in five-card stud poker with nothing wild. It can be done. It is done, more often than most poker players like to admit. However, if you have a nine in the hole and a five, six, and eight showing, you don't bet the deed to the farm on your last card being a seven, no matter *how* lucky you feel. You wait for the next hand—exactly as the frontiersman waited for the target to get closer or stalked closer to it before he fired. In a life-or-death—or a we eat/we don't eat—situation, very few people took unnecessary chances.

The problem with shooting a smaller-caliber round-ball rifle is a physical one, and while we don't understand it fully, we do know pretty much what happens. Any time you have a round object with a sidespin on it—a rifle ball, a golf ball, a baseball, or a ping-pong ball—the ball will often curve in flight in the direction it spins, at a range that depends on its diameter, its weight in relation to its diameter, and the speed with which it is both moving forward and spinning. That's how a pitcher throws a curve ball, what happens when you hook a drive on the golf course, and what happens when you put "english" on a ping-pong ball. It obviously doesn't happen every time—a lot of high, inside pitches that are intended to curve don't—but often enough that shooting a rifle with a round ball beyond 120 yards was chancy. Somewhere around 120 yards the curve in the flight could become so pronounced that the shooter couldn't account for it with the sights, and while the ball would go farther than 120 yards, it couldn't be aimed accurately beyond that distance.

Large-caliber plains rifles, .50s and up, don't seem to have had the problem at all, even with round balls. Round balls, especially in larger calibers, lose velocity very quickly. They probably don't have enough forward speed to curve by the time they've flown 125 to 150 yards. Modern tests with chronographs—electronic instruments that measure the speed of bullets in flight—indicate that large-caliber round balls have lost nearly half their velocity by the time they're 150 yards from the muzzle. Of course, by the time plains rifles came into general use, the round ball was rapidly being replaced in both hunting and warfare by a much more efficient and effective elongated bullet.

This new ball, or bullet, was the result of a lot of experimentation that went into correcting the curve of the shot from the smaller-caliber round-ball rifles. Sam Houston, who was something of a gun tinkerer, designed a rifle in which the grooves and lands were perfectly straight. Sam's idea was to stabilize the ball in the barrel but not spin it so it wouldn't turn in flight. That didn't work as well as he'd hoped it might, but another gunsmith was working on the same problem. In the 1840s, a Frenchman named Minié invented a conical bullet that had a cup-shaped hollow in its base. This new bullet, although not, in fact, an actual ball, was called the Minié ball, and it tended to drift in the direction of the spin the barrel imparted. However, like a football thrown with a spiral pass, it didn't curve in flight. Today the bullets used by the Army in its rifles, pistols, and machine guns aren't balls either, but if they don't explode when they hit, don't set things afire when they hit, and don't leave a trail of smoke, or tracer, behind them in the air, they are called "ball cartridges."

Minié ball used during the Civil War.

The Minié didn't need a patch since it was smaller than the bore and would slide down the barrel easily. When the powder went off, the force of the explosion drove a small wooden or metal plug deeply into the recess in the bottom of the bullet, which expanded the base and made it catch the rifling. Later, the plugs were discarded. They weren't needed anyway, because the force of the explosion was enough to expand the base of the slug. Besides, the force of the explosion sometimes drove the little metal plugs, in particular, completely through the bullet, leaving a ring of lead pressure-welded to the inside of the barrel. This required the ring to be bored out before the gun could be used again.

The Minié was a revolution in long-range rifle shooting. The bullet, being conical rather than round, didn't curve nearly so drastically as a round ball. It did curve, or drift, but the amount was much less than the round ball's curve and it traveled more like a football in a spiral pass. With a Minié-ball load, a man could shoot at a target as far away as four hundred yards—very nearly a quarter mile—and if he had a fine rifle, a steady rest, a perfectly made bullet, and carefully measured, high-quality powder—and, of course, if the day was dead calm—he could actually expect to hit close to his target.

The Minié ball got here a little too late to help at the Alamo, but when it came it stayed a while, and if you take a hard look you'll find that it's still with us. If you take a factory-loaded cartridge for a .45 Colt revolver (what some folks call the .45 Long Colt), one that has the old-fashioned lead bullet with the little bitty flat spot right on the end of it, and pull the bullet out of that cartridge, you'll find that it is a Minié ball, hollow base and all.

A Mexican grenadier of the 1830s, armed with a British Napoleonic-war surplus Brown Bess flintlock musket.

The Texas Revolution was fought exclusively with round-ball guns, and with a few minor exceptions most of them were flintlocks. The Mexican guns, in particular, were guns the Texians, or at least their pappies and grandpappies, knew well already. After all, their dads and granddads had already fought two wars against those guns, one from 1776 to 1781, and one from 1812 to 1814, though the men carrying them in those wars wore red coats and spoke English. When the Napoleonic Wars ended and the British Army switched from flintlocks to percussion or "cap" lock guns, the Crown Arsenal had on hand a lot of Long Land Model Enfield muskets—the gun known as Brown Bess—as well as a lot of flintlock Baker rifles.

A lot of these guns were sold to John Company (the British East India Company) and were used to arm John Company's native army, where they were still shooting as late as the Sepoy Rebellion of 1857. A lot more were sold to the Mexican government after Mexico won her independence in 1821. When Juan Soldado marched mostly barefoot across the brasada of South Texas in that hot February of 1836, the gun he shouldered, like as not, was an English Brown Bess.

After San Jacinto, a lot of those muskets became the property of the fledgling Republic of Texas. They went into the Republic's arsenal, which became the State's arsenal in 1847. In 1861 they were still there. A lot of Texas Confederate Home Guard militiamen shouldered Brown Bess muskets that might well have seen service in the Americas starting in 1775. In 1865 the Yankees confiscated the Texas militia's arsenal; what happened to all those Brown Besses and Baker rifles we don't know.

We call the folks who banded together to fight in the Texas Revolution an army, but it really wasn't. It was a militia:

a band of everything from frontiersmen to shopkeepers who brought whatever rifles, muskets, or shotguns they happened to have when the fight broke out. Just about everything imaginable, from .75-caliber Jaeger rifles and eight-gauge shotguns to pea-ball squirrel rifles, got in the fight, and that hurt.

One of the reasons every country has a special rifle for its army and doesn't just tell all its citizens, "There's going to be a war, bring whatever rifle you happen to have at home so you can get in the army," is so everybody will be using the same caliber and type of ammunition. This is called standardization; with everybody using the same type of rifle and the same kind and caliber of ammunition, resupply is easier. If the battle is on and it will be a while before the supply trucks arrive, soldiers can take unused ammunition from men who have been hurt or killed and keep fighting if they have to.

Texas had no standard guns. In any company of volunteers, the guns might range from a .58-caliber Tennessee punkin-ball hawg rifle to a .28-caliber pea-ball squirrel gun. While the pea-baller and the punkin-baller might exchange powder and maybe flints, the only way the punkin-baller was going to use pea balls was as buckshot. The only way the pea-baller was going to use punkin balls was after he melted them down and remolded them. Our munitions supply in 1836 was a nightmare. If Sam Houston hadn't caught Santa Anna with his pants off at San Jacinto, we probably would have lost the war because of it.

At the Alamo, the Mexican Army quickly learned the limitations of the Americans' long rifles. One of the first things they learned, the hard way, was that showing any kind of reasonable target within that magic 120-yard range of the walls was not a way to live to a ripe old age and get to count

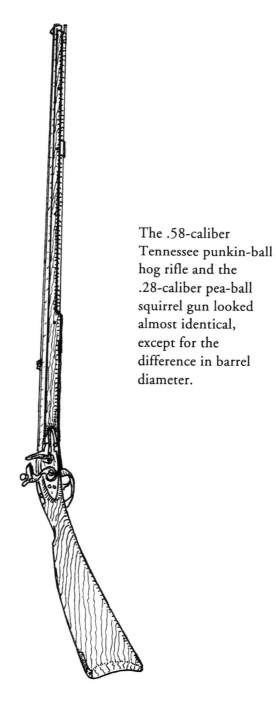

The .58-caliber
Tennessee punkin-ball
hog rifle and the
.28-caliber pea-ball
squirrel gun looked
almost identical,
except for the
difference in barrel
diameter.

your grandchildren. Crockett—they called him Crokey, or perhaps Kwoteky—and his Tennessee riflemen, they quickly learned, were particularly deadly, but beyond about 150 yards they were safe from all but a lucky shot. Santa Anna ordered a cannon moved up to within about two hundred yards of the Alamo and the crew began to batter down a section of the wall, confident that they were out of range of even the celebrated Crokey.

It is a matter of historical record that Crockett and his Tennesseans silenced that gun with rifle fire. It is on that incident that much of the legend of the long-range accuracy of the long rifle and the astounding long-range marksmanship of the Tennesseans is based. There's just one thing wrong with it: it describes something that we know is impossible. Are we dealing with the U.S. Marines here—"The difficult is easy, the impossible takes us a little longer"—or is there another explanation?

What follows is what is known as historical speculation. A better name for it is guesswork. It is, however, educated guesswork based on a knowledge of the weapons and shooting techniques of the time.

David Crockett, though he was by no means a well-educated man, was intelligent. He might never have heard of Agincourt, but that didn't keep him from using just about the same trick the British longbowmen used to destroy a French army, to take out a Mexican cannon five thousand miles to the west and four hundred years later. Davy knew that the gun was out of range for "Old Betsy," at least as far as picking off individual gunners went, but it wasn't out of range for simply dropping a ball in amongst 'em. One ball, that way, had very little chance of hitting anybody. However, a bunch of balls, all coming down pretty much at once and in the same area, was a different story.

Crockett either got a spyglass someplace or picked a man with extremely good eyesight and posted him on the wall along with an excellent rifleman, possibly even Davy himself. The rifleman aimed high and to the left—since the rifling in most long rifles twisted to the right, the bullet would curve to the right—and fired. The spotter watched for the telltale puff of dust on the dry plain.

"Thirty yards this side of 'em, 'bout ten to the right," the spotter called. The rifleman reloaded and aimed at an even greater elevation and farther to the left.

"Looks like ye shot over 'em. Didn't see 'er hit." The rifleman lowered his rifle somewhat.

"Dead on line, just a mite short, maybe five yards." Then eighteen long rifles came up to the same angle—we call it "Tennessee elevation and Kentucky windage" today, meaning an educated guess—and on command all fired at once.

When you come right down to it, the shooting wasn't all that good. Out of a seven-man gun crew, five were hit, which means there were thirteen clean misses. If, however, you have seven men standing around a cannon that is supposed to be well out of rifle range and suddenly five of them are dead, shot down at impossible range by the very rifles that aren't supposed to be able to shoot that far, it is hard to convince the survivors that their survival was due to anything short of the grace of God and the intervention of the Virgin of Guadalupe herself. They are going to tell hair-raising stories of los Tejanos diablos and their terrible long rifles that never miss to their grandchildren. And that, folks, is how legends are born.

The biggest problem with a long rifle, as well as with other weapons of the day, was that it shot once or at most twice and then the shooting was over for a while. A nice long-range rifle is great if there are no more than one or two enemies out there, but opposing armies or Indians didn't often come in ones and twos, they tended to come in bunches. Once a long rifle is empty it doesn't even make a very good club, Fess Parker as Davy Crockett in the Alamo according to Walt Disney notwithstanding. Once the rifle or pistol was empty, the Indian had it all over the white man and his gun.

It takes just under a minute, by actual test, to fire a loaded flintlock long rifle, reload and reprime it, and fire it again with any real hope of putting the second shot in a bull's-eye. That's under ideal conditions, with the rifleman standing up to fire, reload, aim, and fire again, and nobody shooting at him while he does it. Under combat conditions the rifleman lying on his stomach behind a log to fire, rolling on his back to reload while still lying down, then rolling back to fire again, with rifle balls or arrows whanging off the rocks around him or plunking into the log he's using for cover, it takes a while longer.

Once the first shot was fired, the first thing the rifleman did was ground the butt and blow a big puff of wind down the barrel. Remember, from the old cowboy movies, how folks blew the smoke out of their six-shooters? That had a purpose once. Any time you fire a muzzle-loading gun of any sort, there is a chance that some bits of unburned powder or patching material or other trash might linger in the barrel, still smoldering. Dumping a fresh charge of powder down the barrel on top of that live spark could get a mite disconcerting, to say the least. A quick puff of breath went down the muzzle to blow out any possible surprise.

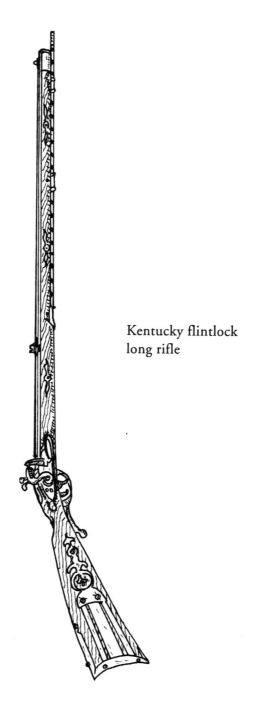

Kentucky flintlock
long rifle

Powder gourd with
wooden spout

The rifleman then poured a fresh charge down the barrel, either from a fancy self-measuring powder flask, or more likely from a powder horn—a hollow cow, sheep, or goat horn full of powder—or a powder gourd, which, cowhorns sometimes being a mite scarce, was a very popular way of carrying powder. Buck Travis, whom schoolbooks call William Barret Travis even though everybody who knew him called him Buck, mentions several times in his diary carrying his powder in a gourd.

Most likely, though, the horn or gourd man poured his powder into a measure, a short tube of brass or horn that contained just the proper charge for Old Thrower, and then poured it down the barrel. There was still a bare chance that he hadn't blown out all the sparks. Since he was holding that horn or gourd containing anywhere from a half-pound to a pound and a half of gunpowder just about in front of his face when he poured, the results of a backflash from the barrel could be hard on a feller, to say the least, if he didn't use a measure.

Once the charge was in, the shooter took a piece of linen, cotton ticking, or thin buckskin, either wiped it across the dob of grease he kept in the patchbox in the butt of his rifle or laid it on his tongue to wet it and make a "spit patch," and laid the patch on the muzzle. He put a ball on it, pressed the ball as far into the muzzle as he could with his thumb, and cut off the rest of the cloth with a sharp knife. Then he pulled four feet of fire-tempered hickory ramrod from its pipes under the barrel. Riflemen always used wooden ramrods, sometimes with brass tips but never steel, as steel could damage the rifling. He put the tip of the rod on the ball and rammed it all the way to the powder with a single stroke. Then if he had time, he bounced the ramrod on the load to make sure it was seated. If it wasn't, the rifle might blow up in his face. If the rod hit with a solid thunk and bounced, the ball was seated. If it hit with a dull, mushy thud and didn't bounce much, he had to ram harder.

Once the rifle was loaded it had to be primed. The shooter opened the pan by tipping the frizzen forward, wiped the pan and frizzen with his thumb to remove any residue from the last shot, checked to make sure the vent—the touch-hole—was clear (if it was clogged he had to clear it with a thin piece of stiff wire called a pick), and poured the pan full of finely ground priming powder from a small priming horn, flask, or gourd. Then he closed the pan, turned the weapon so the lock was up, and shook it or slapped the butt to make sure priming powder entered the vent. That done, he checked to make sure his flint was tight, raised the rifle to his shoulder, cocked the serpentine, drew his bead (took aim), and squeezed her off. By then any Indian who had earned his first feather had gotten to within about ten yards and was busily making the feller look like a pincushion. Like

I said, the Indian had it all over the white man once the rifle was fired.

A lot of men saved their lives in a fight by never firing their rifles. As long as Old Thrower had a ball in the barrel the rifleman was very dangerous, and the Indians knew it. In a lot of cases a single rifleman could face down a half-dozen Indians by keeping his rifle cocked and aimed, without ever pulling the trigger.

A rifleman's idea of a proper load for Old Thrower was one that would "make 'er crack," and any good frontiersman could tell a mile or more away whether a shot he heard was fired from a rifle or a musket. Come to think of it, you still can, if you listen closely. A shotgun or a musket makes a dull booming sound, while a rifle makes a sharp, whip-like crack. Ever wonder why?

That dull boom is the sound of the powder, and a light-loaded rifle sounds just like a shotgun or musket. Only a properly loaded rifle cracks, and while Davy Crockett didn't know why Old Betsy cracked, he knew that when she did the load was right. What makes a rifle crack and what you hear when it cracks is not the sound of the gunpowder, but the sonic boom of the bullet breaking the sound barrier as it comes out of the barrel. Only a rifle shooting a bullet faster than the speed of sound—about twelve hundred feet per second or 750 miles per hour—will crack. Obviously, the heavier the bullet and the larger the caliber of the rifle, the more powder it will take to make 'er crack. While a pea-ball gun might crack with twenty-five or thirty grains of powder, it could take a hundred grains to make a punkin-baller or a .50-caliber plains rifle crack.

Large bore muskets and some large rifles were loaded with cartridges, but the word *cartridge* derives from the Latin

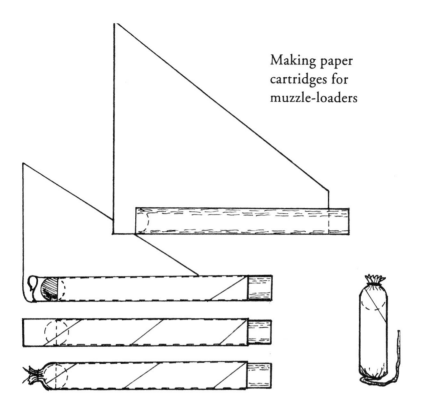

Making paper
cartridges for
muzzle-loaders

word *carta,* which means paper. Early cartridges were pieces of greased or waxed paper, rolled in a tube around a stick slightly smaller than the rifle's bore, one end tied shut with string. The cartridge maker, often the rifleman or musketeer himself, since a lot of cartridges were home-made, slid the wooden former out of a tied cartridge and dropped a ball, a buck and ball load (a ball and three or four buckshot), or a buckshot charge into the paper tube. He put the former back in and tied another string around the bottom of the shot load, pulled out the former, and poured in the powder. Finally he folded or twisted the remaining paper tightly behind the powder charge and bent it over to hold the thing together.

To load a paper cartridge, the rifleman "chawed cartridge" —bit the tail off the paper cartridge—poured the powder down the bore, wadded the paper up under the load, stuffed it in the barrel, and rammed. The waxed or greased paper did duty as a patch. Almost all military weapons used paper cartridges, and you could get turned down for military service if you couldn't chaw cartridge because you were missing a lot of side biting teeth. Believe it or not, as late as 1943, in the middle of World War II, when we were using semiautomatic rifles and machine guns, you could still get rejected for the service if you couldn't chaw cartridge to load a muzzle-loader.

That wax or grease, by the way, once caused a major war. It was usually a mixture of linseed oil and beeswax—the 1847 British regulation specified three pints of linseed oil to a quarter-pound of melted beeswax—but in India, where the native troops were Hindu and Muslim, a rumor arose that the grease was a mixture of hog lard and beef suet. Since Hindus consider cows sacred and won't eat any part of one, and since Muslims consider pigs unclean and won't eat any part of one, the rumor caused some trouble among the native troops of the British East India Company's army. The unrest broke out in open war on Sunday, May 10, 1857, in what is known as the Sepoy Rebellion (native troops were called Sepoys), which was very likely the bloodiest and hardest-fought native war anywhere in the world.

Chapter 4

To Shoot More than Once: Early Breechloaders and Repeaters

There had been attempts for a very long time either to reload faster or to shoot more than once before reloading, and some of these were at least moderately successful. It had been known for a very long time that it was more efficient to load a gun from the back than from the front. Some of the earliest cannons had been breechloaders, with removeable, replaceable, preloaded chambers that were wedged into the weapons' barrels from behind. The idea was a good one, but when corned powder became common, the breechloaders had to be discarded. The more powerful powder put too much strain on the wedges and blew the guns apart.

As early as the sixteenth century, there were experiments with what collectors today call screw-barrel or turn-off pistols. The barrel unscrewed with a sturdy wrench, a charge was dropped into the breech and topped with a ball, and the barrel was screwed back on. Reloading wasn't very fast, but the pistols were amazingly powerful and accurate for the day. Prince Rupert of the Rhine, who fought for King Charles against Cromwell's Parliamentarians in the English Civil War, packed a pair of turn-offs. A shot he made at nearly sixty yards, spinning a weathercock around one way with one pistol and then spinning it the other way with a second shot, is still talked about in England. If you go to the castle where the feat took place, they will still show you the weathercock. With a good pair of binoculars you can see the bullet dents in the head and tail. Most folks weren't that good, but a man armed with a pair of turn-offs could expect to hit a highwayman at thirty or forty yards, which was a lot farther than Dick Turpin could shoot his muzzle-loading pistol or blunderbuss with any accuracy.

Turn-offs stayed around a good many years, and much later some of them were rifled. I've seen a bar-hammer turn-off that dated from the 1840s and was supposed to have been used by a riverboat gambler on the Mississippi. It was double-action, too. All old Deuces Wilde the gambler had to do was pull it out of his coat sleeve and pull the trigger. In all probability a good many turn-offs came to Texas, and it's just possible some are in small county museums, not recognized for what they are. After all, I did once see, in a small county museum, a Sharps Big Fifty buffalo rifle with a thirteen-pound octagonal barrel labeled "old shotgun," so it wouldn't be hard for the folks running a small museum to fail to spot a turn-off.

In the 1760s, a Scotsman named Ferguson, who happened to be a major in the British Army, went the turn-off one better. He built a breechloading flintlock rifle. We're not too concerned with how it worked, since so far as we know no Ferguson rifle ever came to Texas, but as Americans we do need to be glad that there were people on the British Armoury Board (the folks who selected rifles and muskets for the British Army) who didn't like Major Ferguson. You see, Major Ferguson's rifle was not only just as accurate and considerably more powerful than the Kentucky long rifle, it could be reloaded about three times as fast.

The Armoury Board liked the rifle so well it recommended it as the primary weapon for the British Army, and ten thousand of them were ordered. Someone on the Board was jealous of Major Ferguson and removed one zero from the figure, so the British wound up with one thousand rather than ten thousand Ferguson rifles. That may be the reason Old Glory has stars in the field rather than the Union Jack. Had the redcoats been armed with Ferguson rifles rather than Brown Bess muskets, they probably would have made doll rags and kitty litter out of the embattled farmers at Concord and Lexington and ended our revolution before it got going.

In the early nineteenth century, an American named Hall invented another flintlock breechloader. This one had a separate triggering mechanism and chamber, which could be removed from the rifle. You pressed a lever on the bottom of the rifle and the front of the chamber popped up to receive a charge of powder and a ball. No patch, of course, since you didn't have to slide the ball down the barrel. You could load a Hall breechloader about twice as fast as you could a long rifle or a musket. Texas tried to buy some Hall rifles and carbines for its Army, but very few got here because we didn't have any money to pay for them—which we'll get into deeper in Chapter 5. The U.S. Army, however, did use Hall carbines for its Dragoons, which were horse soldiers who did most of their fighting afoot. We didn't have any real cavalry until 1857. This was partially a political choice, since cavalry had always been considered the service for "aristocrats" and

Hall's patented flintlock breechloader with the
breech open for loading. Powder went in, then
the ball, and the breech was closed by pushing
down on it until it locked in place.

America was supposed to be a society without aristocrats, but
expense also was a major consideration. A cavalry regiment
cost at least three times as much to maintain—horses, tack,
saddles, horse feed, veterinary care, and so on—as an infantry regimen. The Hall carbines used by the Dragoons were
percussion, not flint like the illustration above. Apparently
some troopers removed the chamber and firing mechanism
and carried the thing as a pocket pistol at times. Samuel
Chamberlain, who was in the United States Dragoons in the
Mexican War and wrote a book called *My Confession* about
his experiences, mentioned carrying his Hall's carbine chamber as a pocket pistol several times, but he never mentioned
firing it. It's probably just as well. The Hall loaded about
fifty grains of powder and the recoil probably would have
knocked Sam's thumb off when he pulled the trigger.

Sam Houston, who tinkered with guns a lot, designed a multishot rifle with a long magazine machined out of a bar of steel. The gun was percussion, and the chambers were loaded separately, powder and ball, and then capped. The magazine was inserted in one side of the rifle, where it was latched in place. Firing the gun required cocking the hammer, firing, releasing the latch, sliding the magazine over one chamber by hand, relatching, recocking, and firing again. Houston called the thing a harmonica gun, since the magazine, with a little imagination, did look something like a harmonica. It didn't work too well. Not only did all that steel hanging out one side of the rifle or the other tend to unbalance the weapon, but like most early breechloaders it tended to leak a lot of fire where the barrel and chamber joined. This had a bad habit of causing a flashover or chain fire, where the flash leaking out of the junction of chamber and barrel set off another chamber or two. Since the shooter's hand and forearm were in the line of fire if a flashover occurred, guns that tended to flashover weren't too popular with shooters.

The best way to build a gun that shot more than once, most folks decided, was to build more than one gun on a stock. Double-barreled guns—both side-by-side and over-and-under—were popular, but a side-by-side double-barreled gun was very difficult and expensive to build properly. The sights on a side-by-side double-barreled gun were mounted between the barrels, so if the barrels were perfectly parallel the left barrel would always shoot a little to the left of the shooter's target and the right barrel would always shoot a little to the right of it. If the target was a squirrel on a branch seventy yards away, it was possible to have the sights dead on and still miss with both barrels. For that reason, the barrels of a side-by-side double were regulated, set to toe-in just slightly,

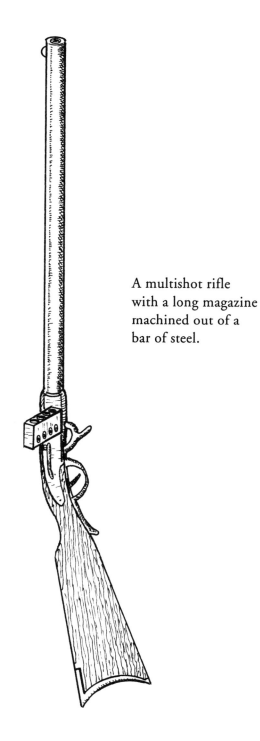

A multishot rifle
with a long magazine
machined out of a
bar of steel.

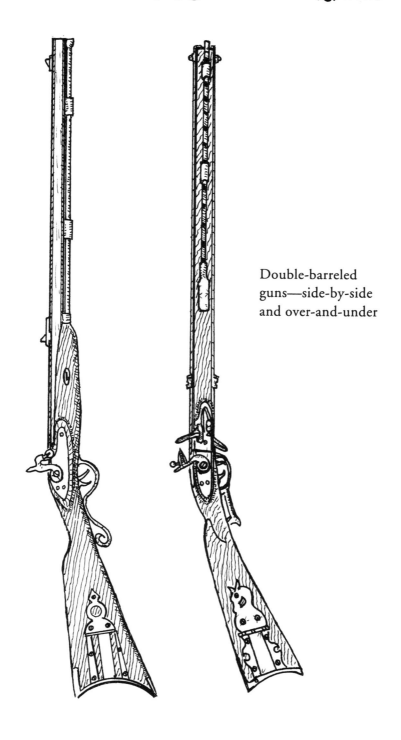

Double-barreled
guns—side-by-side
and over-and-under

so that both barrels would hit the same target at a given distance, which was usually one hundred yards with a rifle or about thirty yards with a shotgun. This toe-in is very, very slight, not visible to the naked eye, and it was also very difficult to get just right. It took a lot of gunsmithing skill to build a side-by-side double rifle, so there weren't many of them and those there were were very expensive. A best-quality single barrel Kentucky or plains rifle might cost a man thirty dollars (gold sold for $5 an ounce at the time), while a double rifle of the same quality might cost one hundred dollars.

Over-under guns were easier to build, but most of them didn't work like modern over-under shotguns. Either they had one hammer coming downward for the top barrel and one coming sideways for the bottom barrel, or the barrels were mounted on a very long swivel screw and the shooter fired the top barrel, then turned the barrels over and fired the bottom one. Both side-by-side and over-under guns were built in flintlock, and an over-under flintlock had two pans and frizzens, but just one serpentine.

On the theory that more is always better, guns with three, four, or even five barrels were built in the same way, but they proved too clumsy and heavy for real use. About the only three-barrel guns left today are the German drillings, which are double-barreled shotguns, usually in sixteen-gauge, with a rifle barrel, usually in 7x57mm R (the equivalent of our .30-.30 Winchester) underneath.

There were others. One French-made gun had a very long barrel indeed, with a series of vents or touch-holes, and a sliding lock. It was loaded with a series of four or five charges, one on top of the other, with thick wadding between. The idea was to fire the front charge, slide the lock back to the next vent, recock and reprime, fire again, and so

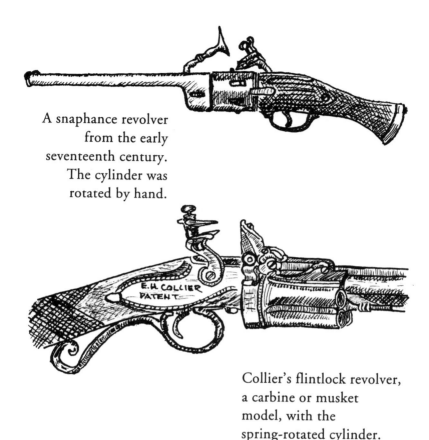

A snaphance revolver from the early seventeenth century. The cylinder was rotated by hand.

Collier's flintlock revolver, a carbine or musket model, with the spring-rotated cylinder.

on. The thick wadding was supposed to keep the gun from letting go everything at once, and it didn't always do what it was supposed to. Besides, if the shooter got excited and slid the lock too far back, firing a charge that wasn't on top, the whole thing would blow apart in his face.

Somebody finally realized that it was better to have five or more short chambers that rotated and a single long barrel, and surprise! his name was not Sam Colt. Guns with a cylinder full of chambers had existed for a very long time, but the chambers were mostly rotated by hand. In the late 1700s, a Yankee named Collier built a flintlock five-shooter pistol on that line, with a cylinder that rotated by a wound-up spring. When you cocked the serpentine and reprimed the gun, the cylinder flipped over to the next loaded chamber and was stopped by a spring-loaded catch called a detent. It didn't always work like Mr. Collier intended, especially when the detent had gotten worn. The pistol would sometimes skip a chamber or two, or even skip them all and spin the cylinder like a top until the spring unwound.

Besides, spring-making being what it was in those days, if you left the pistol wound up all the time the spring tended to set, so when you cocked the gun nothing happened at all. To be on the safe side, you left the spring unwound until the fight was about to start and then took it out and wound it up, which was fine if you saw the fight coming. If you didn't, if you were suddenly confronted by a half dozen street toughs or road agents, or four or five Indians, all bearing down on you with the intent of turning you into buzzard-bait, you had to holler, "Kings X while I wind my pistol up," which probably didn't help too much. The Collier was an interesting mechanical device, but as a pistol a man might have to use to save his life, it didn't work all that well.

Chapter 5

The Percussion Cap
and Sam Colt

The Americans who came to Texas in the 1820s and 1830s brought their guns from home: long rifles and early plains rifles, shotguns, muskets, and pistols, some rifled and some smoothbore. Virtually all of them were flintlock muzzle-loaders. There was, however, at least one percussion, or cap-lock, gun at the Alamo. We know this because the archaeological team that investigated the Alamo in the 1980s and found what has come to be known as the "Alamo skull," also found where some defender had spilled almost a full box of percussion caps. Still, probably 99.99 percent of the guns at both the Alamo and San Jacinto were flintlock, but a revolution in gun making had started in 1807.

Mostly, we don't think of preachers as the sort of folks who experiment with guns, but the Reverend Alexander John Forsythe was a little different. Reverend Forsythe was a Scotsman, and he liked to hunt ducks. And like many educated men of his time, he had a hobby of a technical nature; his happened to be chemistry.

Another Scotsman of the period was noted gunsmith Durs Egg. If you loaded up your double-barreled Durs Egg flintlock fowling piece in a dry place—say, inside a crofter's hut on a hillside far above the loch—and then slipped out in the predawn mist of a Scottish morning to get a shot or two at the ducks as soon as the sun rose, you'd get to shoot exactly twice. Sure, you could reload your fowler with waxed-paper cartridges, and they were at least semi-waterproof, but how could you reprime the pans? Even if you had a tarp or heavy coat to hide under while you did it, the mist would get into the priming powder and get it damp. You couldn't shoot with damp powder.

Reverend Forsythe got tired of going out on the loch, getting two shots at the ducks and maybe missing both times, and then having to row the boat back to shore, climb up the hill to the crofter's hut to reprime in a dry place, and do it all over again after the next time he shot. He began to experiment with a stuff called fulminate of mercury.

Fulminate of mercury will explode if you hit it. Unfortunately, it is very touchy stuff, and sometimes it will explode if you shake it slightly or sneeze close to it. Every now and then it seems to take a notion to explode for no reason that anyone who survives the explosion can remember. It is also extremely powerful. A little bit of fulminate of mercury—say, a daub about as big as the nail on your little finger—if put in a heavy metal spoon and heated over a candle, will blow a hole completely through the spoon. We know this because a man named Samuel Johnson tried it and it worked. A man named James Boswell, who seems to have had nothing better to do with his life than follow Sam Johnson around so he could eventually write a book called *The Life of Samuel Johnson*, told all about it in that tome.

Reverend Forsythe took on the task of taming mercuric fulminate and was successful, at least to the extent that it wouldn't explode if a person sneezed near it. Being a gun tinkerer as well, he built a gun lock to use it. Today we call that lock the Forsythe scent-bottle lock, because it looks a lot like the little perfume bottles ladies used to carry in their reticules. The scent-bottle lock contained enough of the Reverend's tamed fulminate for about a dozen shots. To charge or prime the lock, the shooter turned it upside down, then back right side up. It was fastened to the side of the gun with a hollow screw that served both as a swivel and a touch-hole, and it rotated fairly easily.

The shooter then cocked the gun's hammer—a real hammer at last—aimed, and squeezed her off. The hammer struck a plunger in the top of the scent-bottle lock and fired the priming charge of fulminate by mashing it suddenly. This was called "percussion." Fire squirted through the hollow screw into the chamber, set off the main charge, and the gun fired. There was a one-way valve inside the scent-bottle lock to keep fire away from the rest of the fulminate.

That little valve wasn't always quite as one-way as it was supposed to be. Once in a while it leaked a little fire down into the bottom of the bottle where the spare fulminate was stored. It didn't take much. The scent bottle exploded, tore the side off the gun, and didn't do the shooter a lot of good, either. Reverend Forsythe had a good idea, but he seems to have been better at chemistry and preaching than at gunsmithing.

By 1811, several prominent English and Scottish gunsmiths, among them Joseph Manton and Durs Egg, came out with little copper, brass, or soft iron thimbles about as

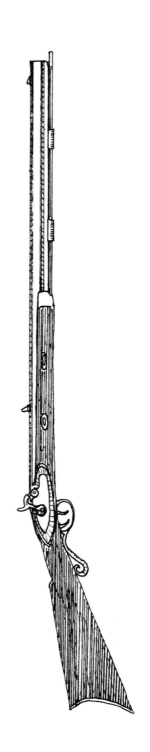

A typical percussion plains rifle from the 1840s-1860s. Note the half stock and a stringer of metal attached to the bottom of the barrel to help stiffen it.

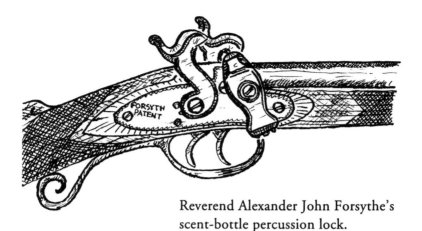

Reverend Alexander John Forsythe's
scent-bottle percussion lock.

big as pencil erasers. They had a small quantity of Reverend
Forsythe's tamed fulminate glued inside. One of these thimbles, or "percussion caps," fitted over a hollow peg called a
nipple, which was screwed into the gun's breech. When the
gun's hammer hit the cap it went "POP!" and squirted fire
into the main charge, firing the gun. This design worked
better than anything, including the wheel lock, ever had before. In an actual test by the British Armoury Board, the
flintlock Brown Bess musket misfired one thousand times in
six thousand shots. The newer percussion gun misfired six
times in six thousand shots. In addition, the caps were pretty
well waterproof, so a gun could be loaded and fired in the
mist, if not in a downpour, without the shooter having to
hunt cover to prime it.

A cap-lock gun had one disadvantage a flintlock didn't.
By the 1830s, caps were very small and easy to carry: one
hundred of them fit in a tin box about as big around as a
modern half-dollar coin and about a half-inch thick. A man
could carry a thousand or more of them without weighing
himself down. But here's the catch. If a man lost his caps,

shot them all up, or got oil on them (and patch grease or natural skin oil would do it), he couldn't shoot any more until he got fresh caps. Oil will kill fulminate of mercury and just about any other percussion priming compound, including modern ones.

A flintlock man, on the other hand, if he was any kind of frontiersman at all, could pick up a chunk of flint, chert, or agate off the ground and knap (chip out) a flint that would work for a few shots, anyway. There's just about no place in Texas you can go that you can't find flint, chert, or agate on the ground if you look hard enough. A cap-lock man was just up that famous creek until he could get more caps. Stores selling percussion caps between, say, San Antonio and El Paso, or up on the Llano Estacado, were awfully scarce for a long time. For that reason it wasn't uncommon to see a frontiersman who packed a pair of cap-lock Colt Dragoon six-shooters who also stuck with his trusty flintlock rifle-gun until away up in the 1850s or even into the 1860s.

By 1811, everything needed to make a cartridge gun existed: technology to make a breechloader and a method of firing the charge without sticking fire to the powder from an outside source. By the early 1830s, a Belgian named Flobert took a huge percussion cap, stuck a big lead BB (actually a .22-caliber lead ball) in the end of it, and built light rifles and pistols to shoot his "Flobert cap." Flobert guns were called "gallery guns" or "parlor guns," and they gave rise to the shooting galleries at carnivals and fairs. At one time it was fashionable to have a target box and a pair of Flobert pistols in the parlor or conservatory of a fine home so the family could practice shooting with the low-powered, not-so-noisy guns. This lasted a long time, for as late as the late 1890s, both Sears, Roebuck and Montgomery Ward were still selling

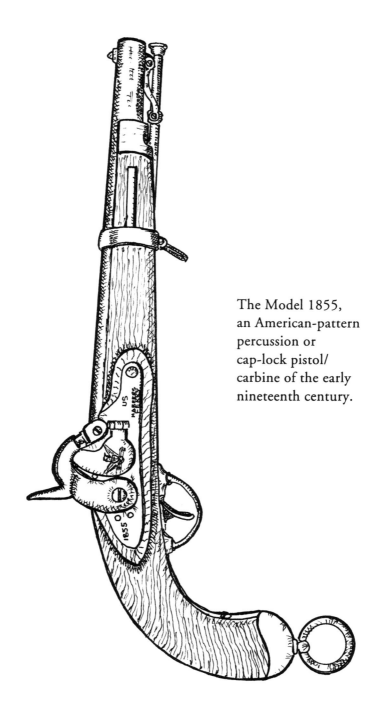

The Model 1855, an American-pattern percussion or cap-lock pistol/carbine of the early nineteenth century.

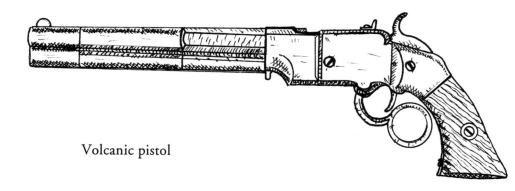

Volcanic pistol

Flobert rifles and ammunition in their mail-order catalogs. Flobert cartridges are still with us, by the way, known today as .22-caliber BB caps or CB caps. They are still very low powered—no powder, just a primer—but out to forty feet or so they are deadly accurate in a single-shot rifle or a revolver. They're just the thing for rats or barn pigeons.

Along in the 1850s, there came on the scene a very peculiar pistol called the Volcanic. It held seven shots in a tubular magazine under the barrel, like the magazine on a lot of modern .22-caliber rifles. It cocked and reloaded by working a finger-lever that also served as a trigger guard, just like a lever-action rifle like the Winchester 94 does today. The Volcanic used a bullet much like a Minié ball but with a deeper hollow in the base. The powder went inside the bullet, and the end was plugged with a cork disk that contained a percussion cap.

The idea sounds good at first; everything goes down the barrel but the remains of the percussion cap. Unfortunately, the people who built the Volcanic didn't realize that a cartridge case has two purposes. One is to make a neat package of primer, powder, and bullet. The main one, though, is to seal the breech of the weapon to keep the shooter from getting a face full of smoke and sparks when the gun is fired. It was a good idea to hold a Volcanic at arm's length and wear goggles when you fired it, because things got a mite hot and smoky around the back end when you touched her off.

The action of the Volcanic was the brainchild of two young men named B. Tyler Henry and Daniel B. Wesson. While the Volcanic wasn't much of a success, it didn't discourage Henry and Wesson from tinkering with guns. Wesson designed a new cartridge, which was a grown-up Flobert cap with more bite in it. It had a copper case with a folded rim like the one on a modern .22 cartridge, and the primer was between the folds on the rim. The case was full of powder and had a bigger bullet in it. When the hammer of the weapon drove a sharp-nosed pin called a firing pin against the breech of the barrel, the rim was in the way. The rim got crushed, which set off the priming compound and fired the powder (rimfire). Wesson then went into partnership with a man named Horace Smith to make pistols for the new cartridge. The company they formed: Smith & Wesson.

Henry continued to tinker with the Volcanic action and rifles. He redesigned it to handle an even larger version of Dan Wesson's grown-up Flobert cap. He added an extractor, which hooked over the fired cartridge's rim and pulled it out of the chamber—the Volcanic hadn't needed one because nothing stayed in the chamber—and an ejector to toss the empty cartridge case clear of the rifle after it was removed from the chamber.

Henry's new gun came out in 1860, shooting a .44-caliber bullet and loading sixteen cartridges in the magazine. A good many Yankees immediately bought Henrys to shoot Confederates with. The poor Johnnie Rebels, who were still having to shove powder and ball down the business ends of their guns, called the Henry "that damn-yankee gun they load on Sunday and shoot all week."

B. Tyler Henry didn't have a lot of money of his own, so he had to get someone to finance his gun factory. The man who did owned a shirt factory. His name was Oliver Winchester. After the war, Winchester took over Henry's gun business entirely and quit making shirts. Today, however, there is still a trace of B. Tyler Henry in Winchester. If you buy a box of modern .22-caliber rimfire cartridges made by Winchester, you'll find that the heads—the bottoms—of the cartridges are stamped with an "H" for B. Tyler Henry, who first invented a repeating rifle to shoot rimfire cartridges.

About 1830 or so, a young merchant seaman named Samuel Colt got the idea for a weapon with a cylindrical, rotating magazine that would shoot several times. The idea wasn't a new one, as we know, but Colt's way of going at it was.

Instead of rotating the cylinder by hand—or with a wound-up spring, like Collier did—Colt decided that the cylinder should be rotated, indexed (each chamber lined up with the barrel), and locked in place when a man cocked the gun. It would all be done with levers and pawls inside the gun, set in motion when the hammer was cocked. There would be no tightly wound spring to be unwound just when it needed to be wound, so the gun would always be ready as soon as trouble started. He claimed he got the idea from a device used to lock a ship's wheel and hold the rudder on a setting.

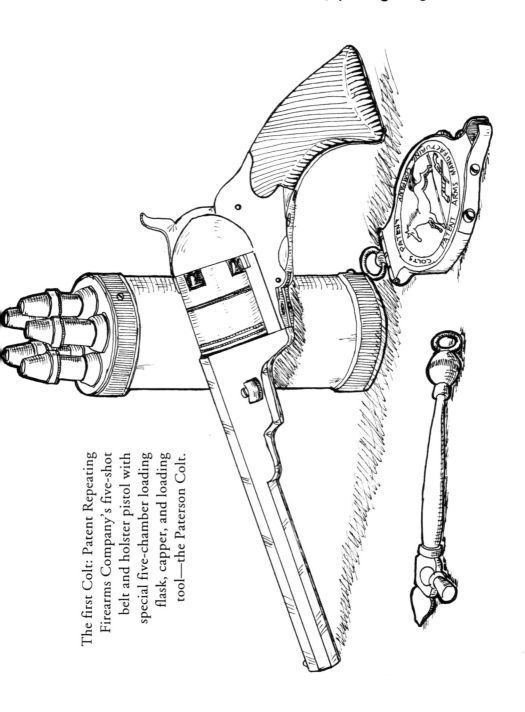

The first Colt: Patent Repeating Firearms Company's five-shot belt and holster pistol with special five-chamber loading flask, capper, and loading tool—the Paterson Colt.

Sam Colt used his merchant seaman's pay to buy a nitrous oxide generating outfit. He toured the northern states as Dr. Coult, traveling to fairs and with medicine shows, demonstrating "the wonder of the age," laughing gas, which supposedly made it painless to pull teeth. By the mid-1830s he had enough money to start work on a patent for his new repeating gun.

On February 23, 1836—on the very day, in fact, that the siege of the Alamo began—Colt filed the papers for his patent. By September he had a patent and established a company called the Patent Repeating Firearms Company in Paterson, New Jersey. Sam Colt was in the business of making guns.

The gun Sam made at Paterson is usually called the Paterson Colt, although it didn't have the famous Colt rearing horse trademark on it, and the only place Sam's name appeared was in the stamping on the barrel, which read: "Colt's Patent, 1836." Colt produced pistols ranging from tiny .28-caliber Baby Paterson pocket models to .36-caliber belt and holster pistols, and several types and calibers of rifles and carbines, all using the same rotating cylinder design.

These new guns loaded from the front just like a muzzleloader: powder first, then an unpatched ball (if the shooter was smart he also put a big daub of axle grease on top of the ball, but it took folks a while to figure that out), and then caps on the nipples screwed in the back of the cylinder. The guns were made in three pieces: the frame and grip on a pistol, or the buttstock and frame on a rifle or carbine, which contained all the working parts and had a long, ungainly looking steel pin with a slot through its outer end sticking out of it; the cylinder, which slid over that pin and had a huge hole in the center of it so it would fit; and the barrel on a pistol, or barrel and forestock on a rifle or carbine. The whole thing was held together with a steel wedge, which slid in a slot in one side of the barrel, went through the slot in the big steel pin, and then came out on the other side of the barrel and held everything together. The action was unnecessarily complicated and delicate, the working parts broke very easily, and all Colt Paterson guns were underpowered for their calibers. They were also the best firearms in the world at the time, but it took Sam a long time to convince folks of that.

Colt sold a lot of guns, both pistols and long guns. George Catlin, the famous painter of Indians, carried a Colt revolving carbine all over the West and the Caribbean in the 1830s and 1840s. A lot of Army and Navy officers bought the repeaters for personal guns, for at that time an officer in the Army or Navy could buy and carry anything he wanted for a personal sidearm. The market Colt really needed—the United States Army and Navy—turned his guns down cold. The weapons, they claimed, were too complicated, too easy to break, and too underpowered; and they were right. They were also the only guns in the world that would shoot five times, rapidly and accurately, without reloading.

In 1839, Sam Colt made the biggest mistake of his life, which in the long run turned out to be the smartest thing he ever did. He sold guns to Texas.

Texas first ruined and later made Sam Colt. Sam's representative brought a suitcase full of samples to the muddy streets of the frontier Republic's new capital, Austin. He demonstrated them for both the Republic's president, Mirabeau B. Lamar, and for the grand old man of Texas politics, Sam Houston. Strangely enough, both men agreed that the new repeaters were just what the Republic needed. I say strangely because Houston and Lamar heartily disliked each other, and it was hard to get them to agree on the time of day when they were both looking at the same sundial.

One man who didn't agree was General George Washington Hockley, the Quartermaster-General of the Republic. It was through Hockley's Quartermaster Department that all military purchases for Texas were supposed to be cleared. George Hockley was an old-line soldier who believed that anything that didn't load from the business end and fire by flint and steel wasn't worthy of being called a gun. To prevent the purchase of the new repeaters, he spent the Republic's entire arms budget for the year in a hurry-up purchase of a bunch of Tryon-made flintlock rifled muskets from Philadelphia which had only been out of date for twenty years.

Little things like not having any money in the treasury never seemed to bother President Lamar, who had been a schoolteacher before coming to Texas and had no real idea where the money to run a government came from. In Alabama, where he'd lived before he came to Texas, there'd always been plenty of "government money." He just didn't realize that in Texas, in the 1830s, things weren't that way. He ordered 250 pistols and 100 carbines from Colt, two hundred pistols and all the carbines to go to the Republic of Texas Regular Army (which existed only on paper and in Lamar's mind), and fifty pistols to go to the much-maligned Texas Navy. Colt agreed to accept four Texas dollars for each U.S. dollar.

About one hundred pistols and thirty carbines had been delivered when Colt shut down the shipments. Texas not only didn't have any real money, it didn't even own the printing press its paper money was printed on. Texas dollars, which Colt had agreed to take at twenty-five cents each, or four for one U.S. dollar, when the contract was signed, had dropped in value to about three cents, or thirty-three for each U.S. dollar, while the shipment was going on and would finally drop to two cents, or fifty per U.S. dollar.

In 1841 Colt went painfully broke, and a lot of the reason for it, though Colt historians don't like to say so, was the big stack of wastepaper Texas paper money Sam collected on the Texas contract. The Paterson factory was auctioned off, and even Sam's personal pair of Paterson pistols were sold. Samuel Colt found himself flat broke and working for the Eli Whitney firm, which made everything from plowpoints and cotton gins to rifled muskets. All Sam had left was his patent, and it would run out in 1857.

Well, there wasn't any Texas Regular Army anywhere but in the President's head and on some planning papers. There were some uniformed hangers-on around the Army headquarters in Austin and some officers who weren't getting any pay but could wear their fancy gold-braided uniforms to parties and dances to impress girls. Even if there had been a regular army, the carbines Texas got from Colt were defective. The cylinders had originally been made for a smaller caliber gun. To make them fit the Texas contract guns, they were heated and reforged to enlarge them. This weakened the cylinders. The first one to be test-fired exploded in the soldier's hands, destroying the gun and tearing his left forearm up. The arm was amputated, but gangrene set into the stump and he died anyway. Texans nicknamed the revolving carbines "Colt's Patent Repeating Wheel Of Misfortune," and it was worth your life to suggest anyone ever shoot another one. The remaining twenty-nine carbines were stored in the old Armory in Austin until the Yankees took them in 1865. Nobody seems to know what happened to them after that.

That bad reputation clung to Colt revolving long guns, although after 1855 Colt made some excellent, reliable revolving rifles and shotguns. They never sold well in Texas, or to Texans wherever they were. No Texan was ever going to shoot another one if he could help it. Colt revolving rifles and shotguns were widely used elsewhere, and from 1861 to 1865 Yankee and Confederate soldiers used them in fairly large numbers to shoot one another, but Texans avoided them. One bad experience was enough, thank you. While they stuck with and swore by Colt pistols for better than a century, they wanted nothing to do with Colt-made revolving rifles or shotguns. To this day Colt revolving longarms are rare in Texas.

Colt's pistols were another story. The Navy got a few, but most of them wound up in the hands of the volunteer Indian-fighting militia called, in those days, the Texian rangers (no capital "R"—the word "Ranger" wasn't officially capitalized until 1880). That, without doubt, was the best thing that ever happened to Sam's pistols (and, just incidentally, to the Texian rangers as well) but it was a few years before that became apparent.

Texas rangers, rough-and-ready Indian fighters in those days and not the lawmen they became later, were the ideal testing ground for the new repeaters, but the first test was less than awe-inspiring. At the Council House fight in San Antonio in 1840, one of the soldiers present when the shooting started pulled his fancy new repeating pistol, took aim at a fleeing Comanche, and pulled the trigger. The barrel fell off. He tried again. The cylinder fell off. He then heaved the rest of the pistol at the Indian, jumped on a horse, ran his man down, and got him with a sword. What had happened, of course, was that the wedge that held the pistol together—and which the experts, rightly, considered the weapon's weakest point—worked loose in the holster and fell out when the pistol was drawn, leaving nothing to hold the gun in one piece.

The Colt Paterson, when you come right down to it, was more of an engineering model than a practical gun. You would be hard put to find a gun less apparently suited to use by hard-riding, hard-fighting irregulars like the rangers of the 1840s. It wasn't very powerful, so you almost had to powder-burn an enemy to be sure you took him out of the fight. It had a peculiar trigger that lay folded up under the frame in a slot machined to hold it, so when the gun was cocked the trigger popped out. It was thin and fragile and broke easily. Once the trigger broke off, a gunsmith had to make a new one or, if no gunsmith was handy, the ranger had to take the gun apart, remove the trigger entirely, and then fire the gun by slip-hammering it, pulling the hammer back with his thumb and letting it go. This was nowhere near as accurate as being able to aim and squeeze a trigger.

There was no trigger guard, which was often the only way to hold on to a gun if you were riding at full gallop in battle and someone, riding full gallop the other way or at right angles to you, slammed into your horse. Some guns, lacking trigger guards, had a swiveled ring set into the butt so a heavy cord or leather thong, also called a "whang," could be used to tie the gun to the shooter and prevent its being lost in a fight, but the Colt didn't have a ring, either. If you lost a Paterson in a fight after 1841, you couldn't get another one, because there weren't any more.

The Paterson had to be taken to pieces to reload it. Most military pistols had come equipped with built-in ramrods for a century or so, but Colt neglected to put one on the Paterson. He did put them on the last Patersons made, in late 1840 and 1841, and if you look at the boxed pair of Paterson Colts in Dr. Goodall Wooten's gun collection in the Texas Memorial Museum in Austin, you'll see they have loading levers, which is what Colt's built-in ramrods are called. Because these pistols have loading levers, and because they are the only Patersons in the museum, a lot of people—assuming, wrongly, that these two pistols are Texas Patersons, part of that original one hundred—have said that the Texas Patersons came equipped with loading levers. This pair of pistols was actually bought in late 1840 by a prominent Texan for his personal use.

The Texas Patersons did come with one spare cylinder per gun, a special powder flask that allowed you to put powder in all five chambers at once, and a special tool that slipped through the slot in the end of the rotating pin and did duty as a ramrod. You could carry two loaded, capped cylinders, and a lot of folks did, but it was risky. It takes just three pounds of pressure, suddenly applied, to fire a cap. If you dropped a cylinder from about waist height onto a rock and it happened to land slightly tilted so a cap struck the rock, the chamber would fire. Recoil would cause it to jump, and if it struck another rock it might well fire again. A dropped cylinder could be a directionally-firing hand grenade that would jump all over the place and fire again and again. If you happened to be in the line of fire, too bad.

Even with all this considered, Paterson Colts were still the best firearms in the world, even a match for the rawhide machine gun that was a Comanche warrior with a bow and a quiver full of arrows (about twenty), and that was what counted. It didn't take long for them to be tested under fire. At Bandera Pass, a little northwest of San Antonio, a war party of Comanches jumped a scout of rangers. The Indians made a feint—a false charge—to draw the fire from the deadly but slow-to-reload rifles, then charged in earnest, expecting to meet only ineffective fire from single-shot pistols and to overwhelm the rangers, whom they outnumbered about six to one.

It didn't quite work out that way. The Comanches charged and were met with a regular hailstorm of lead from the new repeaters. When the smoke cleared, over half the Indians, including the war chief, were dead and the rest were headed for the high lonesome to get away from "guns that speak a time for every finger on a man's hand." The rangers, not yet having invented new ways to fight for their new guns, fought like they had always fought when outnumbered—mountain-man style, putting their backs against something solid where the Indians couldn't get behind them, downing their horses, and letting the Indians come to them. It worked, but for revolvers it was wrong. A revolver in a horseman's hand is a weapon that will carry the fight to the enemy rather than having to wait for the enemy to make the first move.

The man who tested the Patersons best was a short, slim, gray-eyed Tennessean named John Coffee Hays. The Comanches called him "Man-it-is-very-bad-medicine-to-get-in-a-fight-with-because-Devils-help-him" (in Comanche, that's all one word), which is usually shortened to Devil Jack. Devil Jack Hays, pretty much on the spur of the moment, invented the tactics or methods of fighting that were to be used by repeating-pistol-armed light and irregular cavalry for as long as men rode horses in warfare. For nearly a century, almost every great light or irregular cavalry leader who depended mostly on pistols for firepower—men like Jim Lane of Kansas, William Clarke Quantrill and Bill Anderson of Missouri, and John Singleton Mosby of Virginia, to name a few—used the tactics Jack Hays developed on the plains of Texas in 1840 and 1841: stay mounted, charge with your six-shooters blazing, and carry the fight to the enemy rather than waiting for the enemy to come to you.

A few months after the scrap at Bandera Pass, Hays and his ranger company were on scout in what is now Kendall County, west of San Antonio, when they were suckered into a classic "Comanche wheel" ambush. You've seen it many, many times in the movies or on TV: the Indians surround the wagon train or group of soldiers and ride round and round in an ever-tightening circle, shooting, until everyone inside the circle is dead. It had always worked before.

Devil Jack pulled his Patersons and told his men to "powder-burn 'em." Hays had his men carry two revolvers each, which they fired one at a time, holding their horses' reins in their nonshooting hand. The rangers would shoot their revolvers until empty, holster them, and have a fresh gun to fire, not having to stop to reload. The rangers shot their way through, wheeled, hit the survivors from the rear, and shot their way through again. When the smoke cleared, something over half the Comanches and Comancheros (renegade Americans or Mexicans who traded guns and whiskey to the Comanches for slaves and loot taken on raids) were dead in the grass, and the rest were headed for the tall and uncut at a hard run. The rangers lost two men out of twenty, but killed a great many more Comanche and routed the rest. Sam Colt's pistol, complicated, underpowered, and delicate as it was, had proved to be the very best thing ever to happen to the Texas frontier—it and Devil Jack Hays, of course.

Only about half of those early Patersons survived the hard years between 1839 and statehood. When one broke or wore out it was saved, to be cannibalized for parts to repair others. By 1846, when war with Mexico broke out, there were only about fifty working Patersons left in the rangers. They went with the men who volunteered—almost to a man, the whole ranger force—to serve under now-Colonel Jack Hays as mounted scouts for the U.S. Army under General Zachary Taylor.

One of the men who went was a Virginian by birth, a Texian by choice, and a fighting man any way you took him. His name was Samuel Hamilton Walker. As a very young man he'd joined an invasion of Mexico that resulted in the infamous Black Bean drawing at Mier, where he watched a number of his companions shot because they drew black beans in the lottery. Sam had served on the frontier with Hays's rangers, and he knew the value of the repeating pistols. He wanted some for his company of rangers, but Colt was out of business and they weren't available.

Captain Walker proceeded to make a great deal of noise about getting some repeaters, which was heard all the way to Washington, D.C. Congress wouldn't buy the repeaters for just Captain Walker's company, it seemed, but if urged properly it would buy them for the entire ranger force. Captain Walker, joined by Colonel Hays, urged. Sam Walker contacted Sam Colt and the two of them began to correspond about what was needed to build more repeaters.

Colt was working for Eli Whitney. He not only didn't have a factory, he didn't even have one of his own pistols to

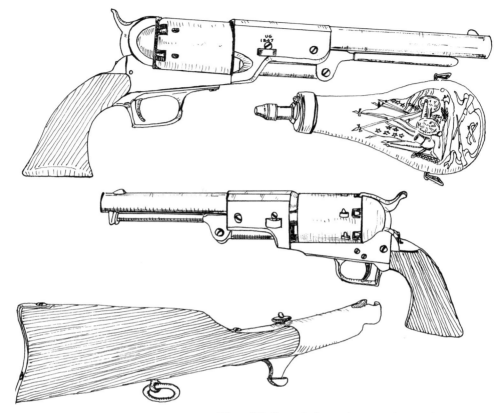

Top, Walker Colt with period powder
flask. Bottom, first model Dragoon
with detachable shoulder stock.

serve as a model. Yet, to his amazement and delight, the very
government that had rejected his guns out of hand in 1839
was now showering him with money to make more guns.
Walker came east to contact Colt, and between them the two
Sams redesigned the repeating pistol.

Sam Walker wanted a he-gun. It had to be a large caliber,
.44 or .45, so when you shot a feller with it he'd know he was

shot right off and not argue about it a while before he found out. To do that, it had to carry a lot of powder, and Sam Walker wanted a *lot* of powder: a whopping big fifty-grain carbine charge. He also wanted a sturdy trigger and a trigger guard to give a feller something to hold onto so he wouldn't drop his pistol in a fight, and a built-in ramrod so you didn't have to take the thing to pieces every time you wanted to load up just one chamber.

He wanted enough weight so the big powder charge and heavy bullet didn't make it try to jump out of a feller's hand every time he let it off, and a long barrel to burn most of the powder so the gun would shoot hard. Most of all, he wanted a simple, rugged action that would stand hard frontier use and wouldn't have to go to a gunsmith every time a feller turned around.

The gun Sam Walker and Sam Colt built is officially known as Colt's First Model Dragoon Revolver, but it is more widely known by other names. One is the Whitneyville Dragoon, because it was made at the Eli Whitney factory (Colt didn't have a factory). The name it's best known by, however, is the Walker Colt, because it was truly more Sam Walker's pistol than Sam Colt's.

You couldn't really call it a pistol, but it didn't have a shoulder stock, so it wasn't a carbine. Perhaps "belt cannon" was a better name for the thing. It was nearly a foot and a half long, had a nine-inch barrel, and weighed more than four and a half pounds unloaded. It was powerful, too. A modern-made replica of a Walker Colt has fired a bullet at a speed of more than 1,500 feet per second (better than one thousand miles per hour), as measured by a chronograph. Before Smith & Wesson built the .44 Magnum revolver in the

1950s, the Walker was the most powerful revolver ever manufactured.

On the minus side, the sights were a low blade in front and a notch in the top of the hammer, visible only when the weapon was cocked, in the rear. If the gun could be carefully aimed, it was deadly accurate on man-sized targets out to seventy-five yards, but the poor sights made careful aiming difficult. It was so heavy that a man had trouble carrying one, let alone two, on his belt without pulling his pants off, so Walkers were generally carried in holsters mounted on a man's saddle.

The loading lever Sam Walker insisted on and Sam Colt had already put on the last model Patersons was held up by a fragile T-spring latch. It was good enough for the low-powered Patersons, but it didn't hold all that well on the powerful Walkers. The blast of firing tended to shake the loading lever loose, so that it fell down, the rammer-end slipped into the bottom chamber, and locked up the gun. If a man saw that happen and had a chance to push it back up, fine. If he didn't, he could be in serious trouble in a fight. In addition, that latch-spring had a bad habit of breaking off. While a gunsmith could replace it fairly easily, you needed both a gunsmith and a spare spring to get it replaced. A lot of Walkers ended the war with their loading-levers tied to their barrels with a piece of string.

Walker Colts, for all their massive size, weren't really all that sturdy. A lot of them blew up at the cylinder. John Salmon "Old Rip" Ford, in his memoirs, claimed the problem was with the new conical bullets. The rangers, so said Old Rip, were unfamiliar with the new bullets and loaded them in the chambers backwards, which caused the guns to explode. From the distance of a century and a quarter, I beg to differ with Rip; but given that Rip Ford was a man of strong opinions, and that he tended to defend his point of view with a six-shooter if he couldn't get it across any other way, that might not be near enough distance. Let me put it like this: I took a modern-made replica of a Walker Colt, crammed nearly sixty grains of powder into each chamber, loaded conical bullets in backwards (which took some doing), capped her up, made sure my earplugs were in tight, and fired her off six times. It was noisy, and I could definitely feel that sixty grains of powder even through more than four and a half pounds of steel, but the pistol showed no signs of blowing up.

Let me suggest another possibility. Walker Colts were made on a military contract, in a hurry, by an outside company that wasn't likely to be making too much on the deal and was, in effect, setting a major competitor up in business. It would be very surprising indeed if some corners weren't cut someplace. The one place corner-cutting wouldn't be noticed right off would be in the quality of the steel. I wouldn't be at all surprised if someday some historian with a scientific bent proved that the cylinders of one batch of Walkers were made of inferior steel and that's why they blew.

There were only eleven hundred Walkers ever made, all at the Eli Whitney factory. A thousand were intended for the troops, two apiece for five hundred men, but only eight hundred ever got there; two hundred were lost when the boat carrying them sank on the Mississippi. One hundred more were what were called civilian models, although rather than selling them outright Colt gave most of them away as promotional pieces. Numbers 1,009 and 1,010 were given to Sam Walker. Of the surviving nine hundred pistols, fewer than two hundred are known to exist today. Since the Walker

Walker Colt was not only Colt's first six-shooter but also the first revolver ever made for the U.S. Army, and was made for the Texas rangers as well, it is extremely valuable today. A rusted-solid Walker with a blown-up cylinder will sell for enough to buy a luxury car, a badly-worn military Walker in working condition will buy a fine house, and a civilian-model Walker in very good condition will allow you to retire early. Now, go take a look at great-granddaddy's old cap-and-ball six-shooter up in the attic, because if it's a Walker you're going to be very, very happy.

Sam Walker was killed at Humantla, in Mexico, shot from ambush after the town had supposedly surrendered. His matched pair of Walker Colts were hanging from his saddlebow when he died. It took a regiment of U.S. Dragoons to corral Walker's ranger company and prevent the Humantla Massacre, for Captain Samuel Walker was well loved by his men. So far as we know, Walker's heirs never got a penny from his redesign of Colt's pistol, but it was a successful redesign. From then on, every Colt single-action revolver ever made, with the sole exception of the Root's Patent models of 1855, used the same action. It is still in use in replicas of Colt single-action revolvers made all over the world.

Colt did make two major alterations in the Walker design almost at once. First, the T-spring that held up the loading lever was replaced by a sturdy latch at the muzzle on all Colt percussion pistols made after 1847. Second, the cylinder was shortened. Never again did any Colt revolver chamber hold more than forty grains of powder. For some reason those cylinders had blown up, and while Sam Colt didn't know why they'd done it, he was determined that no Colt-made revolver would ever do that again. For the record, one did—an all-aluminum revolver Colt made for the U.S. Air

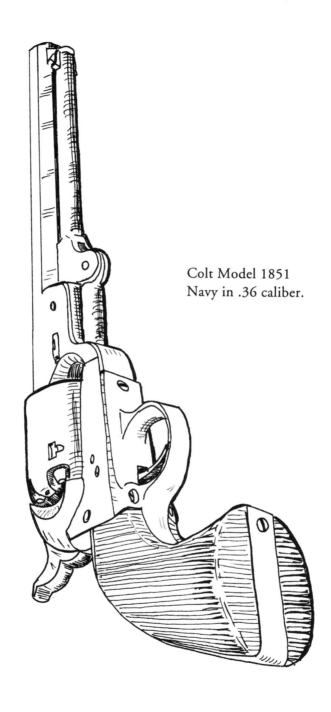

Colt Model 1851
Navy in .36 caliber.

Force in the 1950s—but the fault that time lay in the ammunition used.

Sam Colt never forgot the debt he owed Texas. The engraving on the cylinders of certain Dragoon revolvers showed Texas rangers fighting Indians—although if you didn't know they were supposed to be rangers you couldn't tell, since he's got them in U.S. Dragoon uniforms and rangers have never had uniforms. When Colt brought out the .36-caliber Navy six-shooter in 1851, the cylinder carried a scene of the Texas Navy in battle. Since the 1851 Navy was probably the most widely distributed percussion revolver in history, the Texas Navy is possibly the most widely illustrated navy in the world, and many an Arab sheik, Indian rajah, or later Chinese warlord or Japanese shogun carried, without knowing it, a tribute to the Texas Navy on his engraved, silver-and-gold inlaid Colt Navy six-shooters.

From 1836 until his patent expired, Colt pretty much had the revolver business to himself. There were a few competitors, of course. Some of them made what came to be known as pepperbox pistols, funny-looking things with a very long cylinder that did duty as both cylinder and barrel, sort of like the old multishot rifles. A young man named Sam Clemens, who left his home at Hannibal, Missouri, to go to California and dig for gold, took a pepperbox with him. He wasn't too impressed with how it shot. Years later, in a book called *Roughing It,* Sam Clemens, writing under his pen name Mark Twain, said of a pepperbox: "He aimed the thing at a tree-bole, but fetched the nigh mule."

Pepperboxes were generally small caliber, .25 to .34, and often double-action (all a person had to do was pull the trigger, and the cylinder would rotate, line up, lock, and the hammer would come back and fall). There was no way to put sights on them because they had no barrels. You couldn't really aim a pepperbox, you could only point it. While it might have been fairly effective in a dark alley against a couple of thugs, across a narrow room, or over the width of a poker table, it wasn't much use out in the wide world where folks needed a repeating pistol.

If you wanted a real revolver you had to go to Sam Colt, and most folks wanted one. Colt took out European patents and opened an office in London. Today, in many parts of the world, you can find Colt six-shooters with "Address Colonel Colt, London" stamped on the barrel. Colts went to wars in the United States, Canada, Central and South America, in the deserts of Arabia and the mountains of Afghanistan, on the plains of India, in China, in South Africa, and in a confrontation between settlers and troops in Australia. In fact, the only two large pieces of land on earth on which, so far as anyone knows, Colt revolvers have not fought in wars are the Antarctic continent and the island of Greenland. Just about every other place has heard the bark of a Colt in battle at one time or another.

When Colt's patents finally did expire, just about everybody jumped on the bandwagon. The best early competitor in the United States was the firm of E. Remington and Sons, in Ilion, New York. Eliphalet "Lite" Remington was a gun maker who'd been in business since before Sam Colt went to sea the first time. His guns were and still are fine ones, although the firm of E. Remington and Sons has become Remington Arms Company, Remington-UMC, and Remington-DuPont over the years, and has manufactured such things as typewriters as well as guns. Remington's first step into revolver production was with a fine gun. Remington's designers studied Colt's pistol and decided that they agreed with several

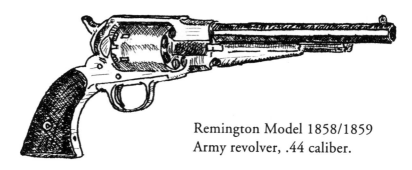

Remington Model 1858/1859
Army revolver, .44 caliber.

years' worth of experts that the Colt design was weak, and the weakness was the three-piece construction and the wedge that held it together. Remington made a one-piece steel frame with a barrel screwed into it, the cylinder protected top and bottom by solid steel straps and pinned in place with a removable spindle. It was a six-shooter, it came in .36 or .44 caliber, and it was solid. You could whack somebody upside the head with a Remington and it wouldn't fall apart. This, the experts back East agreed, was how a revolver should be built.

The real experts on six-shooters were the folks who used them, and most of them stuck with Colt. As soon as a Texan got his hands on a new Colt, he went to a gunsmith and had a new, larger wedge made. He pinned the gun together with the new wedge, driving it in with a blow from the hilt of his knife. He put a preloaded cylinder in his possibles pouch (a leather or canvas shoulder bag that carried all the supplies and tools the gunman could possibly need), and when he shot up his first six, he whacked the wedge out with his knife hilt, stuck it in his mouth, pulled the barrel off and tucked it in his waistband, dropped off the empty cylinder and stuck it in his pocket, slipped the loaded cylinder on the rotating pin and gave it a spin to seat it, stuck the barrel back on, spit out the wedge, slipped it in, gave it a whack to seat it, and presto! he had six more where the first six came from.

A practiced man could change cylinders on a Colt in twenty to thirty seconds, not a lot longer than it takes a policeman to reload his modern revolver. A man armed with a pair of Colts had twelve quick, accurate shots and forty to sixty seconds later he had twelve more. This was great, because with a pair of Colts and a pair of preloaded cylinders, one man could stand off a dozen or more as long as he didn't waste his shots and they didn't sneak up behind him.

A ranger, Indian fighter, lawman, or outlaw was sudden death in all directions for however long it took him to fire two dozen shots. Then all the old problems caught up with him. Revolvers still loaded from the front of the cylinder, loose powder and ball like a long rifle. There's an old joke that insists that the reason gunfights took place at high noon lay in the fact that it took a cap-and-ball man until noon to load his guns and that's if he got an early start.

A man named Rollin White built a ridiculous modification of a Colt in the 1850s. It could never have been used as a serious weapon, but for it to work the cylinder had to be bored all the way through. That's what it takes to load a revolver with cartridge ammunition, but Mr. White never made and probably never intended to make any guns himself. Instead, he licensed his patent to Horace Smith and Daniel B. Wesson. As early as 1858, Smith & Wesson began to build small, pocket-sized revolvers in .22 and .32 rimfire calibers to use the grown-up Flobert caps Dan Wesson developed. Between 1861 and 1865, a lot of them sold to Yankees who felt that they needed more protection than a .58-caliber rifled musket gave them.

Everybody else had to do it the hard way. To load up, a cap and ball man got his powder flask, caps, bullets, a wad of axle grease, and a big rag. He poured a full charge in each chamber—forty grains in a Dragoon, twenty in a Navy—set a ball on top of the chamber, and rammed it in with the geared advantage built into the loading lever. The balls were slightly oversized, so when they were rammed they left a thin ring of lead around the mouth of the chamber, which had to be picked off with a knife. He did this six times, then disassembled the pistol and loaded his spare cylinder. Then, if he was smart, he put a daub of axle grease on top of each ball. This had two purposes: it kept the powder fouling soft and made the gun easier to clean, and it prevented a chain fire. It was impossible to load a cap and ball six-gun with loose powder without getting some powder someplace in the works, and the flash from the first shot would set it off. As long as that's all that happened, fine. Every now and then, though, especially if the mouths of the chambers weren't stuffed with grease, the stray powder would flash over and chain fire, setting off one or two or sometimes all five remaining chambers. It was sort of disconcerting when that happened.

Once the chambers were loaded and greased, the shooter wiped his hands off—remember, oil or grease would kill caps—and put caps on the nipples, carefully lowering the hammer on each one to seat it. If the caps weren't properly seated, they might not fire on the first try.

Finally, he brought the hammer to half-cock, turned the cylinder so that one of the barriers between the nipples was under it, and lowered the hammer. Colt guns had little metal pegs there and a recess in the hammer to fit over them. The combination of peg and hole was supposed to keep the hammer from working its way over to rest on a cap. Remington

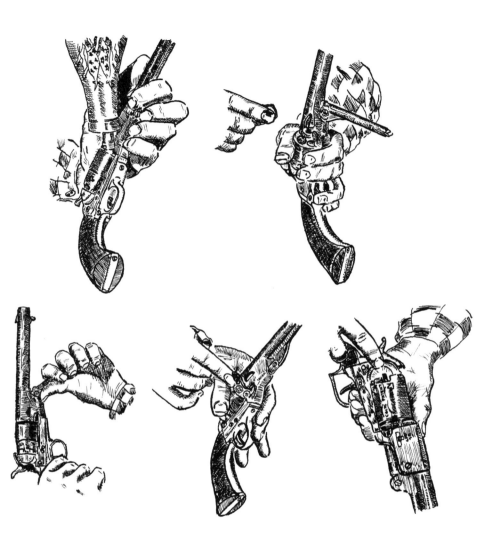

Loading the cap-lock revolver: (1) charging the
chamber; (2) placing the ball; (3) ramming the ball
with the loading lever; (4) greasing the chamber mouth;
(5) capping the chamber. Repeat five to six times to
load the weapon completely.

guns had a wedge-shaped hammer nose and slots between the nipples to lower it into, and that system was much safer than the Colt, because it didn't take long for the Colt pins to wear down to where they didn't hold any more.

It took, you'll remember, just three pounds of pressure to set off a cap, and a lot of accidents happened. In 1866, in Williamson County, just north of Austin, a drover named Harp Perry, on his way to Sedalia, Missouri, with a herd, was saddling his horse in the morning. Like any good cowboy he hung his near stirrup on the saddle horn while he tightened his cinch. When he dropped the stirrup to mount—a thing I've done probably a thousand times or more without getting hurt, and so had he—the falling stirrup struck the hammer on his six-shooter. The hammer was on a cap. The gun fired. The ball went into his leg just above the knee, smashed the knee joint, and broke the big artery in his leg. He bled to death in about fifteen minutes. Some men carried "five beans in the wheel"—five loaded chambers with the hammer resting on an empty—and six loaded chambers in his spare cylinders. Others carried six loaded chambers, but left the one beneath the hammer uncapped, quickly capping it in a fight. Remingtons didn't have to be carried with five beans in the wheel or one uncapped round, but to change cylinders on an early Remington you had to have a screwdriver, so most folks still stuck to Colts.

There were cartridges available for these guns just like there were for rifles, but the cartridges for six-guns were made of thin, chemically treated paper that burned instantly. The paper was made in tubes, with a ball bound in one end with flammable glue, the tube filled with powder, and the open end sealed. To load, you dropped a cartridge into the chamber, bullet end up, rammed, did it five more times, and capped up. Since you weren't pouring loose powder into the chambers, none got into the works, chain fires weren't common, and some folks didn't use grease.

Unfortunately, paper cartridges weren't exactly ideal for the far frontier. Back east, or during a war when they'd be shot up quickly, they were all right, but out west a man might have to ride many a mile—hard, rough riding—before he got to use his paper cartridges. By then they'd been jolted and jounced to pieces in his pouch. In the spring of 1874, just before the U.S. Cavalry got the new Colt cartridge six-shooters, Captain Frederick W. Benteen, who would later command some of the Seventh Cavalry that survived the fight at Little Big Horn, wrote a letter to the Army Ordnance Department. He suggested that any new pistol adopted for the Army use metallic cartridges, since paper ones "tend to go to pieces in the pouch." Fred Benteen had been following "Hard Backsides George" Custer all over the west for about five years. He knew what he was talking about.

In the late 1840s, the U.S. Navy came to Colt for a new pistol for Navy and Marine Corps use. It had to have a brass grip-frame and trigger-guard to keep it from rusting so badly at sea, and the Navy wanted a smaller caliber that didn't use so much powder and lead, probably because a ship at sea is a lot farther from a resupply of powder and lead than is an Army in the field. The pistol Colt built was the 1851 Navy model, .36 caliber, and it became the most popular cap-and-ball six-shooter in the world. Colt's Navy Six was the first full-sized revolver since the Paterson that a man could carry on his belt without being weighed down or having his pants fall off. Unfortunately, it wasn't very powerful; it used only half the powder of the Dragoon or Army pistol, and that worried a lot of folks.

Captain (later Brigadier General) Randolph B. Marcy, in a book called *The Prairie Traveler,* which he wrote in 1859, told about an argument with a grizzly bear. Captain Marcy took a shot at the bear with his rifle and missed, which annoyed the bear. To keep the bear from eating the Captain, empty rifle and all, several young men rode up and shot the animal with Navy six-shooters. As far as Captain Marcy could see, all they did was make the bear madder, and the bear was already mad enough to satisfy the Captain and then some. Finally, someone rode up and shot the bear twice with a Dragoon six-shooter, and it rolled over dead. When it was skinned, the men found that the Navy guns had shot through the bear's hide but the balls had stopped in the thick fat just under the skin. The Dragoon, using twice as much powder, had "penetrated to the beast's vitals" and killed it.

"Thenceforth I resolved," wrote Captain Marcy, "to carry only the Army pistol." A lot of folks felt the same way. While the big Dragoon revolvers were heavier and clumsier than the Navy six-guns, most real frontiersmen stuck by their "trusty .44s." In 1860, Colt brought out a new, lighter, more streamlined pistol, the model 1860 Army. It used the same .44-caliber ball and forty-grain charge as the Dragoons, but weighed only slightly more than the Navy Sixes. It was destined to become very popular. And that, of course, brings us to 1860 and to the end.

Suggested Further Readings

If you are, by now, interested in learning more about guns in American and Texas history, you'll find that there aren't too many books just about guns that aren't full of technical information that might not interest you. That's one of the reasons this book was written.

There are, however, two books that have some information about guns together with a lot of other things which are interesting and one that's just about weapons, and none of them are full of technical information that you have to wade through to get to what you're looking for. Probably the one that has the least information about guns—though it was the first one I ever read that had any information at all about them—is a book called *The Book of Cowboys,* by a man named Holling Clancy Holling. It's an old book, out of print now, and is really a storybook for fourth- to sixth-grade students, but don't let that make you decide not to hunt it out and read it. It's good, and it's fun to read.

The second book, and the most interesting of all, is a book by William Foster-Harris, which is called *The Look of the Old West*. It's not just about guns, although it does have a couple of chapters that deal with them. What it's really about is what the western part of this country looked like before 1900: what people lived in, what they rode in, what they cooked with and what they ate, what they smoked, drank, or chewed, and what they wore and why they wore it. The book is so very good that, a long time ago when there was a TV show called *The $64,000 Question,* this book was used as a reference for answers to questions on the West. *The Look of the Old West* was illustrated by Evelyn Curro, and the drawings are very good, but she has pictures of two revolvers which are labeled "double-action" and they aren't; they're single-action, stud-trigger pocket pistols, of the sort once called "suicide specials."

The third book is called *Weapons,* by Edwin Tunis, and it's probably in your library. It's about just what it says it's about, and it starts with rocks and ends with atomic bombs. The pictures are excellent—Tunis is a great artist and illustrator, and he even puts in cutaway views of the guns so you can see how they worked inside. However, not all the information is accurate, and if you find disagreement between *Weapons* and either *The Look of the Old West* or this book, please believe what Foster-Harris or I tell you, not what you find in the Tunis book. The late William Foster-Harris was, and I am, a western writer. Both of us did a lot of in-depth research into guns that Tunis apparently never did, including going out and firing the guns before writing about them.

Tunis is an illustrator, and a very good one. He's done a lot of books like *Weapons* that are really just picture books that have some information to go with the pictures. In an early edition of *Weapons,* published when I was a teenager, he had a picture of a six-gun, very well drawn, that wasn't any six-gun ever made. I still don't know where he came up with it.

At another point in that edition of *Weapons,* Mr. Tunis said that people sometimes fired revolvers by putting their forefingers alongside the cylinders to help point the weapons accurately, and pulled the triggers with their middle fingers. That tells me Tunis never actually fired a revolver—or at least, not that way. There's a gap—not large but important—between the cylinder and the back end of the barrel on a revolver. Without it, the cylinder won't revolve. When a revolver is fired a lot of fire comes out sideways at that gap. I believed Mr. Tunis—after all, "he wrote the book"—and at about the age of fifteen, I fired a .45 six-shooter with my finger resting alongside the cylinder and fried the end of my forefinger. It still hurts sometimes, when I think about it.

C. F. Eckhardt

Index

Scott, Michael (le Scotte, Michel), 20
scratch flint, 36
screw-barrel, 69
Sears, Roebuck, 86
Sedalia, Missouri, 114
semiautomatic rifles, 66
Sepoy Rebellion, 55, 66
serpentine, 13, 36, 37, 45
Seventh Cavalry, 115
Sharps Big Fifty buffalo rifle, 70
Shawnee, 46
shotgun, 49, 64
side-by-side, 73, 75, 76
slow match, 13, 15, 17–18, 35
Smith & Wesson, 89, 103, 111
Smith, Horace, 89, 111
smokeless gunpowder, 19
snaphance, 36, 39, 43, 77
Spanish foot soldiers, 8, 13, 15–16, 17–18, 25, 28, 55
Spain, 13, 31
Spanish, 3, 5–8, 27, 28, 43
Spanish "Cuera" (leather) Dragoon, 33
Spanish Armada, 26
spanner, 39
Spencer, Christopher, 9
spikes, 37, 39

spit patch, 63
spring-loaded arm, 36
springals, 6
steel, 31, 35, 36, 37
Stinking Springs, 23
sulfur, 8, 19–24
Sulfur Springs, 23
swords, 4, 8

T

Taylor, General Zachary, 101
Tennessee punkin-ball hawg rifle, 56, 57
Texas, 8, 23, 27, 31, 32, 43, 55–56, 70, 81, 86, 94, 95, 108
Texas Confederate Home Guard, 55
Texas Navy, 94
Texas Rangers, 32, 35
Texas Regular Army, 95
Texas Revolution, 55
tomahawks, 45
tompion, 17
touch-hole, 13, 15, 26, 36, 63, 76, 83
Travis, William Barret, 62
trebuchets, 6
triggering mechanism, 13